WUTHERING HEIGHTS

An Anthology of Criticism

Wuthering Heights

An
Anthology of Criticism

Compiled by

ALASTAIR EVERITT

NEW YORK

BARNES & NOBLE, INC.

Publishers · Booksellers · Since 1873

This collection first published in 1967 by   C. /   MAY '68
FRANK CASS AND COMPANY LIMITED
67 Great Russell Street, London WC1

Published in the United States
in 1967
by Barnes & Noble, Inc.
105 Fifth Avenue, New York, N.Y. 10003

Printed in Great Britain

CONTENTS

PREFACE

Wuthering Heights is unique. It hovers in ones imagination and worries for a definition which none seem able to give, and around it has collected the most varied and contradictory criticism. The distinguishing mark of this criticism is dissent, not about the finer points of interpretation but about the essential meaning of the novel, and an awareness of the diversity of this opinion is essential for a realization of the ambiguity and range of *Wuthering Heights*.

The best of this criticism appears for the most part in scholarly journals which often do not form part of school libraries and are certainly inaccessible to the general reader. All that may be consulted is the introduction to the particular edition being used, or the random stimulating essay as that of Lord David Cecil in *Early Victorian Novelists*, or the occasional chapter in general histories. This cannot show the complexity of the novel and it is this very complexity which the present collection wishes to reveal. Also we wish to make conveniently available the classic studies by C. P. Sanger and Leicester Bradner, together with such historically interesting pieces as those by A. Mary F. Robinson and Irene Cooper Willis. There are of course omissions, but this is only meant to be a simple guide and it is questionable whether the majority of readers would require more than this. We only intend to offer sufficient thoughts and suggestions to help the reader decide for himself whether Heathcliff is villain or hero, whether Nellie is admirable or reprehensible, whether the whole book is moral, immoral, or amoral. It is very unlikely that any interpretation here will be completely satisfactory, and as a whole the collection will not provide an ABC or "solution" to the novel.

For those wishing to consult further criticism, more than enough help will be found in the text and footnotes, particularly in Melvin R. Watson's invaluable *"Wuthering Heights* and the Critics." For the Brontë family, *Victorian Fiction: A Guide to Research*, edited by Lionel Stevenson, may be consulted. Perhaps even more important is a visit to Haworth Parsonage, which gives so great an insight into the power of this extraordinary novel.

Finally I wish to thank all contributors, editors and publishers for their co-operation, and in particular F. H. Langman who has made so many valuable suggestions.

A. G. E.

October, 1966.

The Origin of
"Wuthering Heights"*

A. MARY F. ROBINSON

A GREY OLD Parsonage standing among graves, remote from the world on its wind-beaten hill-top, all round the neighbouring summits wild with moors; a lonely place among half-dead ash-trees and stunted thorns, the world cut off on one side by the still ranks of the serried dead, and distanced on the other by mile-long stretches of heath: such, we know, was Emily Brontë's home.

An old, blind, disillusioned father, once prone to an extraordinary violence of temper, but now grown quiet with age, showing his disappointment with life by a melancholy cynicism that was quite sincere; two sisters, both beloved, one, fired with genius and quick to sentiment, hiding her enthusiasm under the cold demeanour of the ex-governess, unsuccessful, and unrecognized; the other gentler, dearer, fairer, slowly dying, inch by inch, of the blighting neighbourhood of vice. One brother, scarce less dear, of set purpose drinking himself to death out of furious thwarted passion for a mistress that he might not marry: these were the members of Emily Brontë's household.

Herself we know: inexperienced, courageous, passionate,

---

* Chapter XIV of A. Mary F. Robinson [Mme. Duclaux], *Emily Brontë* (1883; 2nd ed. 1889).

and full of pity. Was it wonderful that she summed up life in
one bitter line?—

"Conquered good and conquering ill."

Her own circumstances proved the axiom true, and of other
lives she had but little knowledge. Whom should she ask? The
gentle Ellen who seemed of another world, and yet had plentiful troubles of her own? The curates she despised for their
narrow priggishness? The people in the village of whom she
knew nothing save when sickness, wrong, or death summoned
her to their homes to give help and protection? Her life had
given only one view of the world, and she could not realize that
there were others which she had not seen.

"I am bound to avow," says Charlotte, "that she had scarcely
more practical knowledge of the peasantry among whom she
lived than a nun has of the country people that pass her convent
gates. My sister's disposition was not naturally gregarious; circumstances favoured and fostered her tendency to seclusion;
except to go to church, or to take a walk on the hills, she rarely
crossed the threshold of home. Though her feeling for the
people round her was benevolent, intercourse with them she
never sought, nor with very few exceptions, ever experienced;
and yet she knew them, knew their ways, their language, their
family histories; she could hear of them with interest and talk
of them with detail, minute, graphic, and accurate; but with
them she rarely exchanged a word. Hence it ensued that what
her mind had gathered of the real concerning them was too
exclusively confined to those tragic and terrible traits of which,
in listening to the secret annals of every rude vicinage, the
memory is sometimes compelled to receive the impress. Her
imagination, which was a spirit more sombre than sunny, more
powerful than sportive, found in such traits materials whence it
wrought creations like Heathcliff, like Earnshaw, like Cather-

ine. Having formed these beings she did not know what she had done. If the auditors of her work, when read in manuscript, shuddered under the grinding influence of natures so relentless and implacable—of spirits so lost and fallen; if it was complained that the mere hearing of certain vivid and fearful scenes banished sleep by night and disturbed mental peace by day, Ellis Bell would wonder what was meant and suspect the complainant of affectation. Had she but lived, her mind would of itself have grown like a strong tree—loftier and straighter, wider spreading—and its matured fruits would have attained a mellower ripening and sunnier bloom; but on that mind time and experience alone could work, to the influence of other intellects it was not amenable."[1]

Yet no human being is wholly free, none wholly independent, of surroundings. And Emily Brontë least of all could claim such immunity. We can with difficulty just imagine her a prosperous heiress, loving and loved, high-spirited and even hoydenish; but with her cavalier fantasy informed by a gracious splendour all her own, we can just imagine Emily Brontë as Shirley Keeldar, but scarcely Shirley Keeldar writing *Wuthering Heights*. Emily Brontë away from her moors, her loneliness, her poverty, her discipline, her companionship with genius, violence and degradation, would have taken another colour, as hydrangeas grow now red, now blue, according to the nature of the soil. It was not her lack of knowledge of the world that made the novel she wrote become *Wuthering Heights*, not her inexperience, but rather her experience, limited and perverse, indeed, and specialized by a most singular temperament, yet close and very real. Her imagination was as much inspired by the circumstances of her life, as was Anne's when she wrote the *Tenant of Wildfell Hall*, or Charlotte's in her masterpiece *Villette*; but, as in each

---

[1] Charlotte Brontë, *Memoir*.

case the imagination was of a different quality, experience, acting upon it, produced a distinct and dissimilar result; a result
obtained no less by the contrariety than by the harmony of circumstance. For our surroundings affect us in two ways; subtly
and permanently, tingeing us through and through as wine
tinges water, or, by some violent neighbourhood of antipathetic
force, sending us off at a tangent as far as possible from the
antagonistic presence that so detestably environs us. The fact
that Charlotte Brontë knew chiefly clergymen is largely responsible for *Shirley*, that satirical eulogy of the Church and
apotheosis of Sunday-school teachers. But Emily, living in this
same clerical evangelistic atmosphere, is revolted, forced to the
other extreme; and, while sheltering her true opinions from
herself under the all-embracing term "Broad Church," we find
in her writings no belief so strong as the belief in the present
use and glory of life; no love so great as her love for earth—
earth the mother and grave; no assertion of immortality, but a
deep certainty of rest. There is no note so often struck in all her
work, and struck with such variety of emphasis, as this: that
good for goodness' sake is desirable, evil for evil's sake detest-
able, and that for the just and the unjust alike there is rest in the
grave.

This quiet clergyman's daughter, always hearing evil of Dis-
senters, has therefore from pure courage and revolted justice
become a dissenter herself. A dissenter in more ways than one.
Never was a nature more sensitive to the stupidities and narrowness of conventional opinion, a nature more likely to be found
in the ranks of the opposition; and with such a nature indigna-
tion is the force that most often looses the gate of speech. The
impulse to reveal wrongs and sufferings as they really are is
overwhelmingly strong; although the revelation itself be im-
perfect. What, then, would this inexperienced Yorkshire par-
son's daughter reveal? The unlikeness of life to the authorized

pictures of life; the force of evil, only conquerable by the slow-revolving process of nature which admits not the eternal duration of the perverse; the grim and fearful lessons of heredity; the sufficiency of the finite to the finite, of life to life, with no other reward than the conduct of life fulfils to him that lives; the all-penetrating kinship of living things, heather-sprig, singing lark, confident child, relentless tyrant; and, not least, not least to her already in its shadow, the sure and universal peace of death.

A strange evangel from such a preacher; but a faith evermore emphasized and deeper rooted in Emily's mind by her incapacity to acquiesce in the stiff, pragmatic teaching, the narrow prejudice, of the Calvinists of Haworth. Yet this very Calvinism influenced her ideas, this doctrine she so passionately rejected, calling herself a disciple of the tolerant and thoughtful Frederick Maurice, and writing, in defiance of its flames and shriekings, the most soothing consolations to mortality that I remember in our tongue.

Nevertheless, so dual-natured is the force of environment, this antagonistic faith, repelling her to the extreme rebound of belief, did not send her out from it before she had assimilated some of its sternest tenets. From this doctrine of reward and punishment she learned that for every unchecked evil tendency there is a fearful expiation; though she placed it not indeed in the flames of hell, but in the perverted instincts of our own children. Terrible theories of doomed incurable sin and predestined loss warned her that an evil stock will only beget contamination: the children of the mad must be liable to madness; the children of the depraved, bent towards depravity; the seed of the poison-plant springs up to blast and ruin, only to be overcome by uprooting and sterilization, or by the judicious grafting, the patient training of many years.

Thus prejudiced and evangelical Haworth had prepared the

woman who rejected its Hebraic dogma, to find out for herself the underlying truths. She accepted them in their full significance. It has been laid as a blame to her that she nowhere shows any proper abhorrence of the fiendish and vindictive Heathcliff. She who reveals him remembers the dubious parentage of that forsaken seaport baby, "Lascar or Gipsy"; she remembers the Ishmaelitish childhood, too much loved and hated, of the little interloper whose hand was against every man's hand. Remembering this, she submits as patiently to his swarthy soul and savage instincts as to his swarthy skin and "gibberish that nobody could understand." From thistles you gather no grapes.

No use, she seems to be saying, in waiting for the children of evil parents to grow, of their own will and unassisted, straight and noble. The very quality of their will is as inherited as their eyes and hair. Heathcliff is no fiend or goblin; the untrained doomed child of some half-savage sailor's holiday, violent and treacherous. And how far shall we hold the sinner responsible for a nature which is itself the punishment of some forefather's crime. Even for such there must be rest. No possibility in the just and reverent mind of Emily Brontë that the God whom she believed to be the very fount and soul of life could condemn to everlasting fire the victims of morbid tendencies not chosen by themselves. No purgatory, and no everlasting flame, is needed to purify the sins of Heathcliff; his grave on the hillside will grow as green as any other spot of grass, moor-sheep will find the grass as sweet, heath and harebells will grow of the same colour on it as over a baby's grave. For life and sin and punishment end with death to the dying man; he slips his burden then on to other shoulders, and no visions mar his rest.

"I wondered how any one could ever imagine unquiet slumbers for the sleepers in that quiet earth." So ends the last page of *Wuthering Heights*.

So much for the theories of life and evil that the clash of circumstance and character struck out from Emily Brontë. It happened, as we know, that she had occasion to test these theories; and but for that she could never have written *Wuthering Heights*. Not that the story, the conception, would have failed. After all there is nothing more appalling in the violent history of that upland farm than many a midland manor set thick in elms, many a wild country-house of Wales or Cornwall could unfold. Stories more socially painful than the mere brute violence of the Earnshaws; of madness and treachery, stories of girls entrapped unwillingly into a lunatic marriage that the estate might have an heir; legends of fearful violence, of outcast children, dishonoured wives, horrible and persistent evil. Who, in the secret places of his memory, stores not up such haunting gossip? And Emily, familiar with all the wild stories of Haworth for a century back, and nursed on grisly Irish horrors, tales of 1798, tales of oppression and misery, Emily, with all this eerie lore at her finger-ends, would have the less difficulty in combining and working the separate motives into a consistent whole, that she did not know the real people whose histories she knew by heart. No memory of individual manner, dominance or preference for an individual type, caught and disarranged her theories, her conception being the completer from her ignorance. This much her strong reason and her creative power enabled her to effect. But this is not all.

This is the plot; but to make a character speak, act, rave, love, live, die, through a whole lifetime of events, even as the readers feel convinced he must have acted, must have lived and died, this demands at least so much experience of a somewhat similar nature as may serve for a base to one's imagination, a reserve of certainty and reassurance on which to draw in times of perplexity and doubt. Branwell, who sat to Anne sorrily enough for the portrait of Henry Huntingdon, served his sister Emily, not indeed as a model, a thing to copy, but as a chart of proportions by which to measure, and to which to refer, for correct investiture, the inspired idea. Mr. Wemyss Reid (whose great knowledge of the Brontë history and still greater kindness in admitting me to his advantage, as much as might be, I cannot sufficiently acknowledge)—this capable critic perceives a *bona fide* resemblance between the character of Heathcliff and the character of Branwell Brontë as he appeared to his sister Emily. So much, bearing in mind the verse concerning the leveret, I own I cannot see. Branwell seems to me more nearly akin to Heathcliff's miserable son than to Heathcliff. But that, in depicting Heathcliff's outrageous thwarted love for Catherine, Emily did draw upon her experience of her brother's suffering, this extract from an unpublished lecture of Mr. Reid's will sufficiently reveal: [2]

"It was in the enforced companionship of this lost and degraded man that Emily received, I am sure, many of the impressions which were subsequently conveyed to the pages of her book. Has it not been said over and over again by critics of every kind that *Wuthering Heights* reads like the dream of an opium-eater? And here we find that during the whole time of the writing of the book an habitual and avowed opium-eater was at Emily's elbow. I said that perhaps the most striking part of *Wuthering Heights* was that which deals with the relations of Heathcliff and Catherine after she had become the wife of another. Whole pages of the story are filled with the ravings and ragings of the villain against the man whose life stands between him and the woman he loves. Similar ravings are to be found in all the letters of Branwell Brontë written at this period of his career; and we may be sure that similar ravings were always on his lips as, moody and more than half mad, he wandered about the rooms of the parsonage at Haworth. Nay, I have found

---

[2] T. Wemyss Reid, *Emily Brontë*.

some striking verbal coincidences between Branwell's own language and passages in *Wuthering Heights*. In one of his own letters there are these words in reference to the object of his passion: 'My own life without her will be hell. What can the so-called love of her wretched sickly husband be to her compared with mine?' Now, turn to *Wuthering Heights* and you will read these words: 'Two words would comprehend my future—death and hell; existence after losing her would be hell. Yet I was a fool to fancy for a moment that she valued Edgar Linton's attachment more than mine. If he loved with all the powers of his puny being, he couldn't love in eighty years as much as I could in a day.'"

So much share in *Wuthering Heights* Branwell certainly had. He was a page of the book in which his sister studied; he served, as to an artist's temperament all things unconsciously serve, for the rough block of granite out of which the work is hewn, and, even while with difficulty enduring his vices, Emily undoubtedly learned from them those darker secrets of humanity necessary to her tragic incantation. They served her, those dreaded, passionate outbreaks of her brother's, even as the moors she loved, the fancy she courted, served her. Strange divining wand of genius, that conjures gold out of the miriest earth of common life; strange and terrible faculty laying up its stores and half-mechanically drawing its own profit out of our slightest or most miserable experiences noting the gesture with which the mother hears of her son's ruin, catching the faint varying shadow that the white wind-shaken window-blind sends over the dead face by which we watch, drawing its life from a thousand deaths, humiliations, losses, with a hand in our sharpest joys and bitterest sorrows; this faculty was Emily Brontë's, and drew its profit from her brother's shame.

Here ended Branwell's share in producing *Wuthering Heights*. But it is not well to ignore his claim to its entire

B

authorship; for in the contemptuous silence of those who know their falsity, such slanders live and thrive like unclean insects under fallen stones. The vast boast of an unprincipled dreamer, half-mad with opium, half-drunk with gin, meaning nothing but the desire to be admired at any cost, has been given too much prominence by those lovers of sensation who prefer any startling lie to an old truth. Their ranks have been increased by the number of those who, ignorant of the true circumstances of Emily's life, found it impossible that an inexperienced girl could portray so much violence and such morbid passion. On the contrary, given these circumstances, none but a personally inexperienced girl could have treated the subject with the absolute and sexless purity which we find in *Wuthering Heights*. How *infecte*, commonplace, and ignominious would Branwell, relying on his own recollections, have made the thwarted passion of a violent adventurer for a woman whose sickly husband both despise! That purity as of polished steel, as cold and harder than ice, that freedom in dealing with love and hate, as audacious as an infant's love for the bright flame of fire, could only belong to one whose intensity of genius was rivalled by the narrowness of her experience—an experience limited not only by circumstances, but by a nature impervious to any fierier sentiment than the natural love of home and her own people, beginning before remembrance and as unconscious as breathing.

The critic, having Emily's poems and the few remaining verses and letters of Branwell, cannot doubt the incapacity of that unnerved and garrulous prodigal to produce a work of art so sustained, passionate, and remote. For in no respect does the terse, fiery, imaginative style of Emily resemble the weak, disconnected, now vulgar, now pretty mannerisms of Branwell. There is indeed scant evidence that the writer of Emily's poems could produce *Wuthering Heights*; but there is, at any rate, the impossibility that her work could be void of fire, concentration,

and wild fancy. As great an impossibility as that vulgarity and
tawdriness should not obtrude their ugly heads here and there
from under Branwell's finest phrases. And since there is no
single vulgar, trite, or Micawber-like effusion throughout
Wuthering Heights; and since Heathcliff's passion is never
once treated in the despicable would-be worldly fashion in
which Branwell describes his own sensations, and since at the
time that *Wuthering Heights* was written he was manifestly,
and by his own confession, too physically prostrate for any
literary effort, we may conclude that Branwell did not write
the book.

On the other side we have not only the literary evidence of
the similar qualities in *Wuthering Heights* and in the poems of
Ellis Bell, but the express and reiterated assurance of Charlotte
Brontë, who never even dreamed, it would seem, that it could
be supposed her brother wrote the book; the testimony of the
publishers who made their treaty with Ellis Bell; of the servant
Martha who saw her mistress writing it; and—most convincing
of all to those who have appreciated the character of Emily
Brontë—the impossibility that a spirit so upright and so careless
of fame should commit a miserable fraud to obtain it.

Indeed, so baseless is this despicable rumour that to attack it
seems absurd, only sometimes it is wise to risk an absurdity.
Puny insects, left too long unhurt, may turn out dangerous
enemies irretrievably damaging the fertile vine on which they
fastened in the security of their minuteness.

To the three favouring circumstances of Emily's masterpiece,
which we have already mentioned—the neighbourhood of her
home, the character of her disposition, the quality of her experience—a fourth must be added, inferior in degree, and yet
not absolutely unimportant. This is her acquaintance with German literature, and especially with Hoffmann's tales. In Emily
Brontë's day, Romance and Germany had one significance; it

is true that in London and in prose the German influence was
dying out, but in distant Haworth, and in the writings of such
poets as Emily would read, in Scott, in Southey, most of all in
Coleridge, with whose poems her own have so distinct an
affinity, it is still predominant. Of the materialistic influence of
Italy, of atheist Shelley, Byron with his audacity and realism,
sensuous Keats, she would have little experience in her remote
parsonage. And, had she known them, they would probably
have made no impression on a nature only susceptible to kindred
influences. Thackeray, her sister's hero, might have never lived
for all the trace of him we find in Emily's writings; never is
there any single allusion in her work to the most eventful period
of her life, that sight of the lusher fields and taller elms of
middle England; that glimpse of hurrying vast London; that
night on the river, the sun slipping behind the masts, doubly
large through the mist and smoke in which the houses, bridges,
ships are all spectral and dim. No hint of this, nor of the sea,
nor of Belgium, with its quaint foreign life; nor yet of that
French style and method so carefully impressed upon her by
Monsieur Héger, and which so decidedly moulded her elder
sister's art. But in the midst of her business at Haworth we
catch a glimpse of her reading her German book at night, as she
sits on the hearthrug with her arm round Keeper's neck; glancing at it in the kitchen, where she is making bread, with the
volume of her choice propped up before her; and by the style
of the novel jotted down in the rough, almost simultaneously
with her reading, we know that to her the study of German was
not—like French and music—the mere necessary acquirement
of a governess, but an influence that entered her mind and
helped to shape the fashion of her thoughts.

So much preface is necessary to explain, not the genius of
Emily Brontë, but the conditions of that genius—there is no use
saying more. The aim of my writing has been missed if the cir-

cumstances of her career are not present in the mind of my
reader. It is too late at this point to do more than enumerate
them, and briefly point to their significance. Such criticism, in
face of the living work, is all too much like glancing in a green
and beautiful country at a map, from which one may, indeed,
ascertain the roads that lead to it and away, and the size of the
place in relation to surrounding districts, but which can give no
recognizable likeness of the scene which lies all round us, with
its fresh life forgotten and its beauty disregarded. Therefore let
us make an end of theory and turn to the book on which our
heroine's fame is stationed, fronting eternity. It may be that in
unravelling its story and noticing the manner in which its facts
of character and circumstance impressed her mind, we may, for
a moment, be admitted to a more thorough and clearer insight
into its working than we could earn by the completest study of
external evidence, the most earnest and sympathizing criticism.

The Growth of
"Wuthering Heights"*

LEICESTER BRADNER

W HEN *Wuthering Heights* first appeared the immediate
and quite predictable reaction of Victorian readers and reviewers was to view with dismay, if not with disgust, the wildness and brutality of the characters and emotions described in
it. Charlotte Brontë herself, while professing great admiration
for her sister's work, doubted whether it was right to create men
like Heathcliff.[1] Today the wonder of critics is turned upon
another aspect of the book; namely, how could a girl in Emily's
situation, with her limited experience and living her secluded
life, write such a book at all? The researches of biographers
have thrown little light on this problem, largely because of the
very meagre sources to which they may turn. Emily was a
fiercely reticent person. She seems to have had no friends and
hardly any acquaintances outside her family circle. As to people
beyond that circle, Charlotte tells us that "she had scarcely
more knowledge of the peasantry amongst whom she lived than
a nun has of the country people who sometimes pass her convent gates."[2] Her letters and manuscripts were with very few

---

* Reprinted by permission of the Modern Language Association from *PMLA*,
volume XLVIII (1930).
[1] Biographical Notice in 1850 edition of *Wuthering Heights*.
[2] Editor's Preface to 1850 edition.

exceptions—two brief letters and some manuscripts of her poems—destroyed either by Charlotte or herself.

With such a lack of outward evidence it is not surprising that more recent writers, particularly May Sinclair[3] and Romer Wilson,[4] have turned to the record of her imaginative life furnished by the poems. It was pointed out by Miss Sinclair that in the numerous poems devoted to the doings of the Gondals, an imaginary nation created by Emily in childhood but written about in her poetry as late as 1845, we have an unusually powerful treatment of certain themes which are also very prominent in *Wuthering Heights*. Her analysis of the apparent similarity is unfortunately all too brief and she had the disadvantage of writing before the appearance of the important complete edition of Emily Brontë's poems in 1923, which was compiled with the aid of manuscripts unknown to her. Romer Wilson's analysis, very complete in its way, is based on this new edition but is applied only to her explanation of Emily's character. Nevertheless, since this explanation is largely concerned with Heathcliff and Cathy, some light is thrown upon the problem in an indirect way.

It seems desirable, therefore, to present a more extensive survey of those parts of the Gondal cycle of poems which show the early preoccupation of Emily's mind with emotional situations later used in her novel. There are three groups which seem particularly valuable in this connection. The first, a rather mysterious group concerned with children, probably falls entirely within the years 1837 to 1839. The second, certainly written with the same period, is composed of those poems written by a character called A. G. Alaisda or sometimes merely A.G.A. The third group comprises poems by or about the Emperor Julius and his apparently fatal love for Rosina Alcons. These last were

---

[3] *The Three Brontës* (1914).
[4] *All Alone: the Life and Private History of Emily Brontë* (1928).

composed over a period of eight years ending in 1845 and therefore seem to have occupied the writer's mind to a greater extent
than those of the first two groups. Additional proof of this point
is afforded by Anne Brontë's statement in her diary of 1845 that
Emily was writing the life of Emperor Julius.[5] It must not be
supposed that these groups give anything like a complete or
understandable story about the characters contained in them.
They are in the main lyrical rather than narrative, and it is only
by piecing together references to events mentioned in them that
one can arrive at some dim and unsatisfactory glimpses of the
imaginary dramas which Emily was creating in her own mind.
Probably the whole story was told in the "Gondal Chronicles"
also mentioned by Anne, but these, like the life of Emperor
Julius, have not come down to us. One more point remains to
be emphasized, particularly since it has been overlooked by a
number of Brontë students, and I think it is an important point
in the consideration of the growth of her power as a novelist.
This is the fact that many of these poems are dramatic in
nature; that is, it is the characters themselves who are speaking
and not the poet. This is especially to be remembered in the
second group, where A.G.A. is a woman in love with the Lord
of Elbë and not merely a pseudonym for Emily herself as
Romer Wilson supposes.[6]

The poems of childhood are mentioned chiefly because of
their possible connection with the origin of the character of
Heathcliff. The themes are almost entirely tragic and prophesy
a dark and evil fate for a child. A presentiment is felt by the
child itself or by the poet that it is doomed to a life of crime and
misery. One stanza from some verses written in 1837[7] illustrates
the general situation repeated in a number of others:

[5] C. Shorter, *Charlotte Brontë and her Circle*, p. 152.   [6] Particularly pp. 130–131.
[7] *Complete Poems of Emily Jane Brontë*, edited by C. Shorter and C. W. Hatfield
(1923), p. xlviii.

> Darling enthusiast, holy child,
> Too good for this world's warring wild;
> Too heavenly now, but doomed to be
> Hell-like in heart and misery.

This prophecy might well be applied to Heathcliff's career—
although it is hard to think of him as a "holy child." However,
it must be remembered that we know nothing of Heathcliff's
birth and early childhood. Obviously the idea of a harmless and
innocent child growing up to become involved in cruelty and
crime was occupying Emily's mind at this time. In 1839 (Poem
cv) we get the picture reversed, for the subject is a man of dark
crimes who "was once an ardent boy," fond of nature, and the
darling of his mother. The possibility that this group may have
contributed to the development of the Heathcliff theme is
further increased by two undated poems (xxxiv and xxxv)
which in a vague and rudimentary way might be held to fore-
shadow the relations between the outcast Heathcliff and the
heiress Cathy as children. The first describes a "melancholy
boy . . . unblest of heaven" who must undergo a grim fate; in
the second a "child of delight . . . saw and pitied that mourn-
ful boy," and came to love and help him.

There seems to be little to associate this group definitely with
the Gondal cycle, except one poem (cxiv) in which Elbë Hall is
mentioned, and perhaps the poems just discussed did not form
part of that material. There is a great temptation to try to dis-
cern the influence of Wordsworth's poems on childhood here.
It seems pretty certain that the Brontës all read Wordsworth;
for both Charlotte and Branwell wrote letters to him, and he
was later selected as one of the recipients of a copy of the Brontë
poems after the public had refused to buy that volume. Such
verses as those on "The Westmoreland Girl" and "Lucy Gray"
—the latter said by Wordsworth to be a Halifax legend and
therefore perhaps known to Emily already—with their pictures

of wild nature must have appealed to her, as also "We are seven," which would recall the graveyard before her own home and her two dead sisters buried in it. But it is more the tone of certain passages in both poets that suggests the possibility of influence. "Darling enthusiast, holy child" has the ring of the great ode on the Intimations of Immortality, and the following passage from the address to Hartley Coleridge when six years old has a remarkable coincidence of theme and expression with the rest of Emily's quatrain quoted above:

> O blessed vision, happy child!
> Thou art so exquisitely wild,
> I think of thee with many fears
> For what may be thy lot in future years.

And the opening lines of "We are seven"—

> A simple child,
> That lightly draws its breath,
> And feels its life in every limb,
> What should it know of death?

may have had more significance to the darker imagination of a Brontë than we are likely to imagine. Finally, the poem "Her eyes are wild," describing the impetuous ravings of a black-haired mother who came "far from over the main" to her baby boy, may have held her attention, since she herself was to write one (cxii, in 1839) on an outcast mother. The next to the last stanza of Wordsworth's, with its incoherent power and its dark foreboding, has almost the authentic tone of Emily's own work:

> My little babe! thy lips are still,
> And thou hast almost sucked thy fill.
> —Where art thou gone, my own dear child?
> What wicked looks are those I see?
> Alas! Alas! that look so wild,
> It never, never came from me.

Leaving these poems, their relation to the so-called Gondal cycle being somewhat obscure, we now turn to that cycle itself. Of the two groups previously referred to, the Alaisda or Elbë poems certainly ceased to be written six years earlier than the last of the Julius poems, and would seem to be less central. They begin in August, 1837, with a poem signed A.G.A., in which the writer mourns the exile of Alexander, Lord of Elbë, who is on the desolate sea, "Thinking of Gondal and grieving for me." The next two poems in the series (LVII and CXX) show A.G.A. despairing and in prison. In February 1838 appears a poem headed in one manuscript "Lines by A.G.A. to A.S." which contains two significant stanzas:

> Call Death—yes, Death, he is thine own—
>   The grave shall close those limbs around,
> And hush, forever hush the tone
>   I loved above all earthly sound.
>
> . . . .
>
> If thou hast sinned in this world of care,
>   Twas but the dust of thy drear abode:
> Thy soul was pure when it entered here,
>   And pure it will go again to God.

Taken in connection with the other poems by A.G.A. (LXXVII, XCIV, CVI), which are uniformly despairing in mood, and with an unsigned poem of 1838 (LXXXIX) describing Elbë Hall in ruins, this would seem to indicate that "A.S." is Alexander, the Lord of Elbë mentioned in the first poem. The "S." I have not been able to expand. Alexander, then, is another dark-souled hero, a grown-up version of the child already discussed. In poem LXXVII (May, 1838) we have a mysterious reference to a noble foe who had once been a priceless friend to her. Though signed A.G.A., it is hard to say whether the speaker here is thinking of Alexander or some other character in the story Emily was creating. Since her heroes and heroines pretty uniformly betray each other, this would not prevent the possibility that Alexander is referred to. This is all the plot material, if it may be called such, discoverable in the A.G.A. group. It would seem to be the story of the love of A. G. Alaisda for the Lord of Elbë, who perhaps later became her "noble foe" and at any rate was exiled from his home. He dies, and she is left to grieve for him and defend his character.

The story of Emperor Julius and Rosina Alcons, as gathered from the poems, is similar but more fully expanded, possibly because the poems were composed over a period more than twice as long. In December, 1837, several months after the first A.G.A. poem, we find the title "Song by Julius Angora." His army has been given the victory, the crimson ensign is triumphant over the "sea-green standard." The mention of "nations resting round" who are obviously involved in the battle gives a hint that Julius' war was more than merely a struggle between two nations. The battle of Waterloo may have served as a model. In March, 1838, we find Gondal's monarchs (evidently Gondal, at this time at any rate, comprised more than one country) swearing never-dying union. Julius, however, "blasts with that oath his perjured soul," and burning thoughts "kindle a short and bitter smile" on his face as he clasps Gerald's hand. In May, 1838, a poem called "Gleneden's Dream" contains a vision of an avenging hand striking down in the midst of his retainers a tyrant whose ambition has drained Gondal of her life blood and the lives of her noblest sons. It seems as if France and Napoleon must have suggested this situation. In April, 1839, we find that that is exactly what has happened to Julius. A little over two years later Rosina Alcons, who must have been in the story all the time, first appears to the reader of the poems. On this occasion she is recovering from a long and delirious illness. She seems to think that there has been a revolution in Julius' empire but that he has subdued it and reigns secure again. She learns, however, what we already know, that Julius has been killed within his own palace by an assassin:

> And now, mid northern mountains alone,
>   His desert grave is made;
> And, lady, of your love alone
>   Remains a mortal shade!

In November, 1844, is a poem called "Love's Rebuke" which goes back to a period before Julius' death. He has suffered some unnamed reverse of fortune for which he reproaches Rosina, beginning:

> Rosina, this had never been
> Except for you, my dearest queen!

Except for her, he says, he would be on his way to southern isles across the sea.[8] He says he knows her "haughty beauty's sovereignty," that he has read her eyes and feels it is not love they reveal.

> They flash, they burn with lightning shine;
> But not with such fond fire as mine;
> The tender star fades faint and wan
> Before Ambition's scorching sun.
> So deem I now; and time will prove
> If I have wronged Rosina's love.

Combining this with "Gleneden's Dream," I am inclined to believe that in the complete story Julius has been driven by Rosina's ambition to commit some act of oppression and tyranny which finally brought about his doom. Nevertheless time did prove that he had wronged Rosina's love, even though he may have been right as to her ambition. In the following year Emily caused Rosina to address to the memory of Julius one of the most passionate expressions of enduring love ever penned, the poem long known as "Remembrance."

---

[8] For some hints on the location of places in the Gondal poems see Miss Ratchford's article "The Brontës' Web of Dreams," *Yale Review*, XXI, esp. pp. 155–156. Miss Ratchford has examined Anne Brontë's pencilled notes in the family geography.

Cold in the earth—and fifteen wild Decembers
  From those brown hills have melted into spring
Faithful indeed is the spirit that remembers
  After such years of change and suffering!
.   .   .   .
All my life's bliss from thy dear life was given,
  All my life's bliss is in the grave with thee.

It seems probable that during the eight years Emily was composing these poems several different versions of the Julius story
may have commended themselves to her mind. For instance in
1839 we find a poem called "Lines by Claudia" in which she
laments the death of her monarch who

died to rule forever
A heart that can forget him never.

One stanza runs:

Yet if the soul can thus return,
I need not, and I will not mourn;
  And vainly did you drive me far
With leagues of ocean stretched between:
  My mortal flesh you might debar,
But not the eternal fire within.

In all this we see almost an exact parallel to the situation of
Rosina and are led to suspect that Claudia may at one time have
occupied Rosina's place in the story, since the latter's name does
not occur till 1841. The separation by ocean should be compared
with Julius' remarks in his poem last referred to concerning the
southern isles. Again in Poem cxxxiv we find a lament for a
departed lover who lies buried in a foreign land and whose
enemies have traduced his memory. It concludes:

What have I dreamt? *He* lies asleep,
With whom my heart would vainly weep:
He rests, and *I* endure the woe
That left his spirit long ago.

This seems very close in situation and spirit to Rosina's case. It also seems probable that "Light up thy halls" (Poem xcvii), long hailed as one of Emily's best poems and already associated by several writers with the spirit of *Wuthering Heights*, is connected with some version of the Julius story. This version, however, must have been an early one (the poem was written in November, 1838), for in it the writer, who is a man, commits suicide, whereas it is established in three poems that Julius was murdered. Nevertheless, the relations between the writer of "Light up thy halls" and the haughty lady of his love, who is in a "far land" while he is in a cold and dreary region of Gondal, are very similar to those between Julius and Rosina just before his death. Some estrangement has taken place and the writer feels that

> could she see me now, perchance her lip would smile,
> Would smile in careless pride and utter scorn the while!
> But yet for all her hate, each parting glance would tell
> A stronger passion breathed, burned in this last farewell;
> Unconquered in my soul the Tyrant rules me still;
> *Life* bows to my control, but *Love* I cannot kill!

Romer Wilson, in developing her idea of the importance of the "dark hero" in Emily's imagination, suggests the examples she had in the preceding generation of Byron and Napoleon.[9] Certainly there is much of Napoleon in Julius' career—there seems to be even a suspicion that he was not a Gondal by birth, just as Napoleon was not French—and there is certainly much of the Byronic hero in his character. Through the intermediate step of Julius, and allowing for obvious differences in situation, it is not improbable that some traces of the gigantic figures of the emperor and the poet are present in the dark sins and almost incredible successes of Heathcliff.

---

[9] *All Alone*, pp. 113–116.

It now remains to sum up the elements in all of Emily's poetry which may throw light on the genesis of *Wuthering Heights*. First, as we have already seen, the poems about a doomed child show that the child grows up into a character like Heathcliff and they also show, in one poem, a forecast of the childhood love of Heathcliff and Cathy. In the A.G.A. poems we have the theme of sin and exile combined with the laments of the surviving lover for the one who is dead. In the much more important Julius group appear two characters who must, in the complete story, have been highly developed and individualized. Julius and Rosina were apparently both proud and intractable, like Heathcliff and Cathy. Rosina, like Cathy, causes trouble by her ambition; Julius, like Heathcliff, is beset with sin and a tyrannical spirit. Then comes Julius' death, followed by long years of life for Rosina during which the memory of her lover is always poignantly with her. Here, as in the A.G.A. poems, it should be noticed that it is the woman who survives and mourns the man. Though Emily put something of herself into the lovers of both sexes, it is usually the woman into whose mouth she puts her finest poetry and through whose feelings she can best express her grief for a departed lover. Many examples of this could be cited; the only important exception is "Light up thy halls." The changing of the sexes in this relationship in the novel can, I think, be explained by other influences to be mentioned later. It is not to be supposed, of course, that Emily had any thoughts of writing a novel at the time that the main outlines of these stories took shape, though we know that she later wrote the life of Emperor Julius. Nevertheless, by the creating of these personages of her imaginary world and by the building up of careers full of passionate intensity for them she was unconsciously preparing herself for the writing of *Wuthering Heights*.

II

It is clear, then, that most of the important emotional themes and situations in *Wuthering Heights* had already been developed in Emily's mind before 1840 and one of these situations had in 1845 formed the substance of her greatest poem—*Remembrance*. But the Gondal poems form a narrative of empire, martial glory, war, imprisonment, defeat, despair, etc., having as characters emperors, lords, rebel leaders, queens, and ladies of high rank. They may account for the emotions in the novel, but not for the plot and persons. Where did Emily Brontë acquire the material for the harsh brutalities so vividly presented in her story? One would naturally suppose that her observation of the people of her own Haworth region might have given it to her were it not for Charlotte's emphatic statements on this point. Charlotte qualifies them, however, by saying that although Emily knew nothing of them personally, she liked to hear about them and all their affairs, and that it thus came about that she received an unduly large proportion of the tragic and terrible tales always current in "the secret annals of every rude vicinage."[10] Yet one feels that Charlotte, who was in reality somewhat shocked herself by *Wuthering Heights*, is here merely trying to make excuses for her dead sister against the objections of the reviewers. She mentions no specific local tales that could have suggested Heathcliff and Cathy nor have later writers told us of any in the vicinity of Haworth. Dr. Wright tries to supply the lack of local legends by tales of Irish life which Emily is supposed to have heard from her father.[11] This theory was successfully quashed by Clement Shorter, who not only pointed out many inconsistencies in it but also learned from Miss Nussey and Mr. Nicholls that neither of them ever heard a word from Mr. Brontë or his daughters about these Irish

---

[10] Editor's Preface to *Wuthering Heights*.
[11] William Wright, *The Brontës in Ireland* (1893).

C

stories.[12] However, in another quarter, the search for local
stories has apparently been more successful. Mr. Charles Simpson, in his recent book on Emily Brontë,[13] has investigated a
field left largely untouched by her previous biographers. For a
period variously estimated from eight months to two years
Emily was a teacher at Miss Patchett's school at Law Hill near
Halifax. Mr. Simpson's researches show not only that there was
a servant named Mrs. Earnshaw at the school during her stay,
that certain grotesque carvings over the gate of a near-by hall
probably suggested the description of the carvings over the door
at Wuthering Heights, and that there are a few similarities in
details of setting, but also that a bit of recent local family history
bears a number of strong resemblances to the life of Heathcliff.
Summarized briefly, the story is as follows. John Walker, of
Waterclough Hall in Southowram, has adopted his nephew,
Jack Sharp. Jack "abused his uncle's kindness, developed an
overbearing and unscrupulous character, and gradually possessed himself of the main interests in the business" of his uncle.
Walker's oldest son took no part in the business, so when the
second son died and Walker retired and left the district Sharp
remained in possession of the business and the Hall. In 1771 the
oldest son married and gave his cousin notice to quit the Hall.
The son arrived with a charming wife, but his estate was mortgaged and the Hall badly in disrepair, only two rooms being
suitably furnished. Her character triumphed, nevertheless, over
all difficulties, and they managed to retain their place in local
society. Jack Sharp took his ill-gotten gains and built Law Hill,
the house in which Miss Patchett's school was later located.

This story of the cuckoo in the nest certainly has a strong
resemblance to the relations of Heathcliff to the Earnshaw
family, so strong that it is almost impossible to deny that it must

---

[12] *Charlotte Brontë and her Circle*, pp. 157–158.
[13] *Emily Brontë* (1929).

have been in part at least the source of that element of the plot of *Wuthering Heights*. The close association of the story with the house in which Emily was living makes it equally probable that she could not have escaped hearing it. The years 1837–38 were, as shown by her poetry, years during which her imagination was very much aroused and the fact that it was during this period that she heard of the events connected with Jack Sharp would have aided in etching them powerfully on her memory. However, we must notice that, although Heathcliff in his practice of unscrupulous usurpation parallels the career of Sharp, in character and motives he is very different. The latter is, as far as Mr. Simpson's summary reveals, merely a rather crafty and disagreeable business man, who was after one of the family. This is far removed from the romantic intensity and the mad combination of love and revenge which drives Heathcliff from one cruelty to another. For all of Heathcliff's character and all that it means to the novel we find no source in the story of Jack Sharp.

This completes the evidence drawn by writers on the Brontës from any of the known experiences of Emily herself. There remains, finally, the question of her reading. It would seem on the face of it that the reading of a girl whose life was as devoid of incident as Emily's is said to have been might easily exert a large influence on any novel she might write, that is as to plot at any rate. And, in fact, exactly this claim has been made by Mrs. Humphrey Ward[14] and more recently by Romer Wilson.[15] The former pointed out the probability that the romantic subject matter of Hoffmann's tales influenced Emily, but Romer Wilson pinned it down to one story, *The Entail (Das Majorat)*. It is well known that the sisters read a good deal of German while at Brussels, and a comparison of this tale with *Wuthering*

---

[14] Thornfield Edition of *Wuthering Heights* (Harper and Bros., 1900), Preface.
[15] *All Alone*, p. 248.

Heights leaves little doubt that Emily read it. Hoffmann describes a lonely half-ruined castle by the sea, around which the wind sweeps and whistles desolately. It is owned by a family with a tragic secret in its past. An old lawyer, for many years their trusted counsellor, brings his young nephew with him on a visit of business. They arrive on a cold night to find the gates locked, and are admitted only after great shouting and hallooing. In the sitting room assigned to them the nephew notices a bricked-up doorway in the wall, but thinks little of it at the time. Before going to bed, he amuses himself by reading one of Schiller's ghost stories. Suddenly he is startled by the blowing open of the door, followed by a sound of footsteps and of sighs and moans expressive of the deepest and most hopeless grief. After this, a frantic scratching is heard on the bricked-up doorway. These sounds, we learn later, were made by the ghost of old Daniel, a servant who many years ago had murdered an heir to the estate by pushing him through that doorway. The rest of the story, with its account of the nephew's violently romantic love for the wife of the present Baron and the long reminiscence of family history by the old lawyer, is much too extended to be summarized here.

Romer Wilson maintains that the framework of *Wuthering Heights* was "borrowed outright" from Hoffmann's tale.[16] This is a claim which a comparison of the two plots will hardly support. The mere fact that there are orphan heirs and heiresses and an usurper in both stories is not of great importance when we find that there is almost no real similarity between the history of the Earnshaw family and that of the barons of Roland-sitten. There are, however, other kinds of borrowing which one must immediately grant. That the opening events of Emily's story was taken from the *Entail* seems to me quite certain, par-

---

[16] *All Alone*, p. 248.

ticularly the reading of a book at night followed by the appearance of a ghost which makes scratching noises, and so also was the device of having the story told as a reminiscence of an old and faithful servant of the family. Nor will anyone be likely to deny the claim that Hoffmann's crabbedly loyal Daniel inspired the creation of Joseph. Yet here we must notice an important difference. Daniel committed a murder and plays an important part in the plot; Joseph is a superb piece of characterization but has only a very minor role in *Wuthering Heights*. In other words, what *Wuthering Heights* owes to the *Entail* is not the conception of its plot, certainly one of the most potent elements of Emily's book, but a definite selection of several of the opening scenes, one device of story telling (that of having events related by an old servant to someone previously unconnected with the family), and one character, who is reduced from his position of plot importance to that of a finely executed but certainly minor personality, a sort of gargoyle.

Up to the present it does not seem to have occurred to anyone to examine the files of *Blackwood's Magazine*, that ever-present literary guide and political mentor of the whole Brontë family. Now it happens that in November, 1840, a time when we know Emily was at home, there appeared in *Blackwood's* a story of twenty-four closely printed pages entitled *The Bridegroom of Barna*.[17] It was printed anonymously, both in the magazine and in the collection called *Tales from Blackwood*. The scene is laid in Ireland and the two main characters are a beautiful girl of good family and her lover, the orphan heir to a fine bit of farming country. The girl's family disapproved of the match, with the result that her brother forced a duel upon Lawlor, the lover. The brother was dangerously wounded and Lawlor fled the country for a time. However, before long the brother dies,

[17] XLVIII, 680–704.

although not of the wound, and so does the girl's mother. The father, unable to stand the strain of seeing his daughter sinking day by day under her grief at being separated from her lover, finally agrees to permit the match. On the day of the wedding, an enemy reveals to the police that Lawlor was the ringleader in a brutal gang murder of two years previous, and he is obliged to fly for his life on his own wedding night. Ellen, prostrated by the shock of learning of her lover's crime, revives after some months to a state of languid resignation. Then one summer night, Hugh suddenly returns, risking his life in eluding the p⌐lice agents watching the house for just this event. There follows a scene which, in its passionate intensity, equals the return of Heathcliff after Cathy's illness. When Ellen reproaches him for endangering his life, he replies: "Oh, darling! what have I not dared in this world and the next, to be forever within sight of the beauty from which I am debarred forever? Yet one hour with you, only *one hour*, Ellen, were it but once in the long dreary year, and I could bear to live." The police raid the house just after Lawlor, with the aid of an old fortune teller, has made his escape, but Ellen is thrown by the shock into a delirious fever. Though surviving this, her constitution has suffered too much to live long, and in the following spring she died and was buried in the old churchyard of Abbeymahon.

Three days after her interment the same man who had betrayed Lawlor on his wedding night came to the police and offered to show them where the outlaw could be captured. Leading them through miles of mountain bogs and moorlands, he finally stationed them at the edge of the Abbeymahon graveyard. "By the side of Ellen Nugent's new-made grave sat the murderer Lawlor, enclosing in his arms the form that had once comprised all earth's love and beauty for him, and which, like a miser, with wild and maniac affection, he unburied once more to clasp and contemplate. The shroud had fallen from the upper part of the body upon which decay had as yet made slight impression. The delicate head lay reclined upon that shoulder which had been its home so often, and over which now streamed the long bright hair like a flood of loosened gold, the wan face turned up to his as if it still could thrill to the mad kisses in which he steeped it, while he had twined one of the white arms frantically about his neck." Lawlor addresses passionate words of love and pleas for forgiveness to Ellen's corpse, but is interrupted in the midst of them by the entrance of the police, who shoot him dead at the same moment that he opens fire on them. The story concludes with the following lines. "Hugh Lawlor was the last of his family, and his corpse was unclaimed by friend or relative; but the strangers who dug his grave did not venture to separate in death the hapless pair who in life could never be united."

No summary can give an idea of the wild scenery of the Irish hills and the many details of the brutality of the lives of the Irish country people found in this unusual story. Much less well done from a literary point of view, they nevertheless present some similarity to the parallel elements in *Wuthering Heights*. Far more important, however, are certain matters of plot and character. First, it is said that the young man was savage and cross to everyone except Ellen. Second, the orphaned condition of Lawlor and the fact that he and Ellen Nugent had been lovers since childhood are particularly mentioned in the story. Third, his absence and return are of considerable importance on two occasions, the second return being a contributory cause to the death of his beloved. Fourth, the disinterring of the girl by her lover, and fifth, the final common grave for both. These points are too numerous and too close to the corresponding parts of Emily's plot to have been mere coincidence. Consciously or unconsciously she made use of them as important parts of her structure. Furthermore, in the character of Hugh Lawlor we

have most of the elements of Heathcliff's personality which
were missing in Jack Sharp, particularly the wildness, brutality,
and passionate intensity. The most striking divergence is in the
character of Ellen, who not only does not give up her lover for a
richer man but shows none of Cathy's traits at all, being meek,
long-suffering, and religious. But considering everything, *The
Bridegroom of Barna* must be held to be a much more important piece of source material than *The Entail*. The kind of life
described in it is much closer to that of the Yorkshire moors
and the character of Lawlor is much more like Heathcliff than
anyone in Hoffmann's tale.

III

Let us now recapitulate the evidence which has been accumu-
lated in the preceding pages. As early as the years 1837 to 1839
the beginnings of what was to be Heathcliff's character and of his
relationship to Cathy may be discerned in the poetry, and from
1839 to 1845 the development of the character of Rosina makes
this even clearer. At the same time that these first beginnings of
the Heathcliff idea appear in the poems, Emily became ac-
quainted with the story of Jack Sharp, the overbearing and unprincipled usurper. In 1840 she read *The Bridegroom of Barna*
in *Blackwood's*; in 1842 she read Hoffmann's story, presumably
while studying German in Brussels. During all this time we
have not the slightest evidence that she ever considered writing
a novel, in the ordinary sense of the word. Therefore, it is impossible to speak of her novel as a direct imitation of those
works. She simply read them as she would anything else, as
Coleridge read all the mass of items recorded by Professor
Lowes, and when the time came to write *Wuthering Heights*
they made themselves felt because of some unconscious appeal
they had made long ago to her thoughts and emotions.
In the meantime Emily had been acquiring practice in

writing narrative in prose. In 1841 she and Anne had begun the Gondal chronicles, which must have contained much material about Julius and Rosina as well as the other romantic adventurers of that exciting land. Finally in July, 1845, Anne records in her diary that "Emily is engaged in writing the Emperor Julius's life. She has read some of it and I want very much to hear the rest." The reworking of Julius's story into a separate book, with all its artistic problems increased by its independence from the rest of the chronicle, must have greatly developed its author's powers as a narrator and may have had something to do with that steady flow of events and remarkable unity of tone which characterizes her published novel. Whether Anne ever saw the rest of this life of Julius, or indeed whether Emily ever brought it to completion, is not recorded, nor has any later eye seen the manuscript. It is supposed that Charlotte, or even more probably Emily herself, destroyed it.

Up to this time the Gondal game had been the private imaginings of Emily and Anne, and the Gondal poetry had been private to Emily alone. Anne had known of it but never seen it. Now in 1845 Charlotte came across some of Emily's poetry, including many of these Gondal poems, and was filled with an ambitious desire to publish it along with her own and Anne's. Emily was highly incensed at this intrusion on her innermost thoughts and only with the greatest difficulty was persuaded to allow the publication of the poems. From this time on no more is heard of Emperor Julius and the Gondals. Knowing the fierce reticence of Emily's nature, injured now by this chance discovery, we can imagine that his name never crossed her lips again. At any rate, two results of this event are seen in the following year. Emily fell in, apparently without any demurring, to the plan that each should write a novel, and the novel, when written, was as different from life among the Gondals as could be imagined. Gone are the noble heroes and fine ladies, gone are the empires and revolutions. Of everything in the lives of Julius and Rosina there remains only the passionate intensity with which they loved and thwarted each other, that intensity which makes "Remembrance," even to those ignorant of the story behind it, one of the most powerful poems in our language. That remains, and with it some of the things most intimately connected with their characters—the sins of Julius and the ambition of Rosina.

We have no means of knowing what were Emily's ideals for the form and content of a novel when that momentous decision was made that each of the sisters should write one. We only know that in regard to the subject matter suitable for such a work she was no subscriber to Victorian delicacy of taste; in fact, she seemed to have no conception that any such limits were to be observed. Charlotte apologetically records this attitude in her preface. "If the auditor of her work, when read in manuscript, shuddered under the grinding influence of natures so relentless and implacable, of spirit so lost and fallen; if it was complained that the mere hearing of certain vivid and fearful scenes banished sleep by night, and disturbed mental peace by day, Ellis Bell would wonder what was meant, and suspect the complainant of affectation." Of her reading in fiction we have but few traces. Scott was an early favourite, but outside of his peasantry he could have had little influence on *Wuthering Heights*, though he doubtless is responsible for much in the Gondal chronicles. The stories in *Blackwood's* were too miscellaneous in type to have exerted any definite effect, and the tales of the German romantics, read at Brussels and in various translations appearing in *Blackwood's*, would have given her examples of wild emotion but very little in the way of form and structure. Dickens, if she read him, would have provided an example of a popular author not afraid to deal with downright vice and brutality, though he certainly would never have asso-

ciated these qualities with his heroes. The descriptions of hard-
ness, tenacity, and family feuds in the Scotch novels of John
Galt would have provided more suggestions for *Wuthering
Heights*, but again it is impossible to say whether they came to
Emily's attention.

Romer Wilson believes that Emily started out to write a tale,[18]
in imitation of Hoffmann's type of story, rather than a novel,
but does not attempt to explain how the change came about.
The knowledge we now have that *The Bridegroom of Barna*
was also a source would seem to confirm this theory, since the
latter story is even shorter than *The Entail*. However, it is difficult to imagine that so good a craftsman as Emily showed herself to be could have been misled in this way very long. Even if
the original conception of the plot had only extended to the
deaths of Catherine and her brother, that section of the present
book would in itself be almost of novel length. She may have
thought at first of composing a tale of tragic intensity which
should involve Linton, Heathcliff, and Cathy in a swift and
violent catastrophe on the return of the deserted lover, a tale
similar to *The Bridegroom of Barna* in length and rapidity of
action. If this was the case, she either discarded it completely
after trying the plan or else the pull of the Jack Sharp story with
its slow theme of usurpation and recovery or the descent of
action through several generations in Hoffmann or both of
them together made themselves felt and altered her conception
of her scheme before any important crisis was reached. Without the continuation of the story into the next generation there
would have been little point in carefully providing all the important characters with offspring. The birth of Hareton occurs
less than a quarter of the way through the book; at the halfway
point the second Catherine is born, and shortly after, Linton

[18] *All Alone*, p. 250.

Heathcliff. The main point of Hindley's marriage and of Heathcliff's is to provide new characters who will be useful in the second part of the story. Cathy's child, as it is partially responsible for her death, might have been retained had the plot been restricted to the form of a tale, but there would have been no reason for the others. Furthermore, the opening of the story as it stands implies everything that has taken place in the first half of the plot. This method of beginning *medias in res*, which she probably borrowed from *The Entail*, shows that the whole story had been planned before she began to write it in its present form. Everything seems to me to indicate that it never had any other form. The other two sisters wrote novels, not tales, and there is no reason that Emily should have been an exception. Nor can I see any traces of an earlier, shorter conception cropping up in the book. The careful working out of every detail, the beautiful structural symmetry of the whole, leave no room for such a theory. Emily's artistic judgment, unlike Charlotte's, was equal to her inspiration.

It seems to me evident from what we know of Emily that she never considered using the Gondals in her novel. They were too private and personal matter to be dealt out to the public for cash. But Julius and Rosina were ghosts too potent to be abjured so easily. Sternly banished in their original regality, they reappear on the Yorkshire moors none the less imperious for the rough garb they wear. They must, however, have a plot in which to act out their "eternal passion and eternal pain." We have seen that it was not borrowed wholesale from Hoffmann. It contains materials from many sources, some of which must always remain undiscovered. For the setting she must have unhesitatingly, one would suppose, chosen her native moors, and this choice would have determined some further elements. It would have necessitated the use of the rough country folk of whom Charlotte tells us she had heard so many tragic stories.

The location of some two houses within her own knowledge may have suggested the relationship of Wuthering Heights and Thrushcross Grange, and it is very probable that at this point the memory of Jack Sharp and his two houses came into her mind and suggested to her the theme of usurpation. Whether the similarity of her setting with the wildness of the country in *The Entail* reminded her of the indirect narration in that story, or whether her realization of the desirability of such a method for her story brought Hoffmann to mind, is unimportant. What is important is her realization, however obtained, that an account of such violent passions and brutal cruelties can be endured by the reader much better if they are told as having happened in the past. Never was Wordsworth's "emotion recollected in tranquillity" better illustrated. Nellie Dean, kind-hearted but placid in her feelings, independent of the family but united to it by ties of loyalty, is exactly the person to tell the story of the fate of the Earnshaws.

It is when we come to Julius in his new aspect and what the character of this new Julius is to mean to the book that the importance of *The Bridegroom of Barna* is apparent. Hugh Lawlor presents the elements of intensity and brutality which Jack Sharp lacked. It is evident from the close similarity of parts of his career with those of Heathcliff that he must have been definitely chosen as the model for Emily's new hero. Heathcliff is much more fully developed in every way, but his literary ancestry seems to be very clearly that of a combination of Emperor Julius and Hugh Lawlor. This perhaps helps to explain the shift in sex from the situation in the Gondal saga where the woman survives the man. Lawlor had been the cause of Ellen Nugent's death, had survived her, and had opened her grave. This same sequence is repeated in *Wuthering Heights*. Another cause may also be suggested. Emily's story was to be one of brutal revenge on the part of the survivor, and it would have been difficult if not impossible to carry this out had Cathy survived Heathcliff. These two influences may have exerted themselves more or less simultaneously. In whatever way it is regarded, it seems to me that the entrance of the spirit of Julius into the outward semblance of Hugh Lawlor and the association of this new character with the general trend of events in the career of Jack Sharp form the backbone of *Wuthering Heights*.

In the case of Cathy there was apparently no such complex development. In none of the stories mentioned is there any character remotely resembling her. Cathy is Emily Brontë's supreme and original creation. She dominates the spirit of the book as Heathcliff dominates its form. Probably she is largely fashioned out of Rosina, whose impetuous pride and ambition she possesses. In her the wild and tameless soul of her creator flamed into life—into a life not bounded by cooking and ironing and learning German but free and uncontrollable, Emily at her imaginary best and worst, the spirit of Byronic revolt invested with a new and strange power by the winds of the moor. It is Cathy's spirit reacting upon Heathcliff, and not Heathcliff himself, that makes *Wuthering Heights* memorable.

It is not to be supposed that the foregoing discussion is intended to "explain" a great and somewhat mystic book nor to reduce genius to a series of sources. I have simply attempted to show how the imagination of a poet, who for once turned novelist, has fused together into perfect synthesis a number of raw materials existing in her mind. Much undoubtedly will always remain unknown, particularly about the Gondals, but it is none the less worth while to reconstruct, even partially, the growth of a masterpiece.

"Wuthering Heights" and the Critics*

MELVIN R. WATSON

Wuthering heights is now generally acknowledged to be one of the greatest English novels, but it has gained this recognition only after a battle with the critics and general public which has lasted a large part of the hundred years since its publication. It seems proper, therefore, to study this body of criticism and appreciation with several questions in mind: How much is there? What different attitudes have been shown towards the book and its author? How rational and penetrating have the comments been? What reasons have been given for its greatness? How much attention has been paid to interpreting *Wuthering Heights* as a work of art and how much merely to appreciation or to side issues?[1]

Certain themes appear often enough to provide a series of leit-motifs in this critical opera. "Forcible writing," "powerful and original," "awkwardly and illogically constructed"—these run right through the comments, with scarcely a dissenting

---

* © 1949 by The Regents of the University of California. Reprinted from *Nineteenth-Century Fiction*, Vol. III, pp. 243–263, by permission of The Regents.

[1] The emphasis throughout this study is on *Wuthering Heights*, not on Emily Brontë or her family. Furthermore, no attempt has been made to discuss every comment or even every essay. In treating the material of the past few decades I have perforce been more selective than in dealing with nineteenth-century notices; I believe, however, that the examples chosen are typical.

voice. Many feel compelled to compare Emily to Charlotte and *Wuthering Heights* to *Jane Eyre*, with the foregone conclusion that Charlotte and *Jane Eyre* are superior. "The work of immature genius," shouts a chorus. The early charge of "unnatural passion" (made by a contemporary reviewer) is essentially repeated in the "dominant sexuality" which, according to a French writer, pervades the entire book. Hysterical, delirious, nightmarish, primeval, and elemental—all these are used in describing the book. Comparisons with Elizabethan tragedies and characters are frequent and not always complimentary: it is compared with *Hamlet*, but also with *Titus Andronicus*; Heathcliff resembles Hamlet, but he is also the greatest villain since Iago. Its authorship has been attributed to both Charlotte and Branwell; Heathcliff has been considered both protagonist and villain. Finally, the novel as a work of art has been considered a "burden of absurdities" and the "one perfect work of art amid all the vast varied canvasses of Victorian fiction."

From a study of this sort the first conclusion that emerges is that *Wuthering Heights* was not so completely neglected on its appearance as has often been assumed. To the five newspaper reviews found in Emily's writing desk in Haworth Parsonage I have been able to add a number, especially from monthly magazines. But the picture of almost complete critical disapproval is merely filled in by these. The most favourable is the unidentified review, which Emily must have cherished:

One of the most interesting stories we have read for many a long day. . . . It is not every day that so good a novel makes its appearance; and to give its contents in detail would be depriving many a reader of half the delight he would experience from the perusal of the work itself. To its pages we must refer him then; there he will have ample opportunity of sympathising . . . with the feelings of childhood, youth, manhood, and age, and all the emotions and passions which agitate the restless bosom of humanity.[2]

---

[2] Quoted from Charles Simpson, *Emily Brontë* (London: Country Life, 1929), pp. 178–179.

Perhaps this reviewer had not read the book carefully; at any rate the other contemporary notices, though less complimentary, are less general and more pointed in their comments, the *Spectator*, for example, contending that *Wuthering Heights* attempts

to give novelty and interest to fiction, by resorting to those singular "characters" that used to exist everywhere, but especially in retired and remote country places. The success is not equal to the abilities of the writer; chiefly because the incidents and persons are too coarse and disagreeable to be attractive, the very best being improbable with a moral taint about them, and the villainy not leading to results sufficient to justify the elaborate pains taken in depicting it. The execution, however, is good: grant the writer all that is requisite as regards matter, and the delineation is forceful and truthful.[3]

Two longer newspaper reviews both succumb to its "rugged power" and "unconscious strength," but object at great length to the wildness, strangeness, painfulness of the story; to its lack of relief; to the ferocity and inconsistency, the lack of *vraisemblance* in Heathcliff; to the confusion in the artistic technique; and to the contemptibleness of all the characters.[4] Even less sympathetic than these, however, are some of the contemporary notices. One writer asserted that "it should have been called *Withering Heights*, for anything from which the mind and body could more instinctively shrink, than the mansion and its tenants, cannot be easily imagined"; and the august *Quarterly* blasted both *Jane Eyre* and *Wuthering Heights* thus: "Though there is a decided family likeness between the two, yet the aspect of the Jane and Rochester animals in their native state, as Catherine and Heathfield [*sic*], is too odiously and abominably pagan to be palatable even to the most vitiated class of English readers."[5] Because *Wuthering Heights* did not conform

---

[3] *Spectator*, XX (1847), 1217.
[4] *Atlas*, XXIII (1848), 59; and *Examiner*, January 8, 1848, pp. 21–22.
[5] *New Monthly Magazine and Humourist*, LXXXII (1848), 140; and *Quarterly Review*, LXXXIV (1848), 175.

D

to the accepted standards of Victorian novel writing, it was condemned by yet another magazine. Because the novel neither teaches "mankind to avoid one course and take another" nor dissects "any portion of existing society, exhibiting together its weak and strong points," its powerful writing was thrown away.[6] Tait's reviewer was also the first to point to one technical problem which was not solved for many years, the legality of the manner in which Heathcliff gained possession of both Wuthering Heights and Thrushcross Grange.

But two American journals gave *Wuthering Heights* its longest reviews. Furthermore, if one can believe the implications of these articles, the novel had been more of a popular success here than in England. "G.W.P.," writing in the *American Review*, devoted almost fifteen pages to the book in the hope that he could counteract the bad influence which it had exerted; and more explicitly, the critic for the *North American Review* insisted, perhaps a bit too optimistically, that this fiction had cured the "Jane Eyre fever" and "ended the last desperate attempt to corrupt the virtue of the sturdy descendants of the Puritans." Both, as usual, admit the immense power of the book; but one attacks primarily the coarseness of language and manners and the untruthfulness of the passions exhibited, and the other denounces the brutality and spiritual wickedness of the main character.[7]

Nor did the second edition, famous for Charlotte's preface,[8] provoke any reviews which showed more complete understanding. Though the *Athenaeum* accepts it as "a more than usually interesting contribution to the history of female authorship in

---

[6] *Tait's Edinburgh Magazine*, XV (1848), 138.

[7] *American Review*, VII (1848), 572–585; *North American Review*, LXVII (1848), 354–360. The last is a group review of a half-dozen or so novels.

[8] No matter how sincere her intentions, Charlotte showed little comprehension of the true greatness of the book, for the general tone of the work, especially the superhuman strength of Heathcliff, disturbed her as much as it had any of her contemporaries. Echoes of this preface are often heard in later years.

England," the *Eclectic Review* characterizes it as a "repellent book," in which the powers are "not only premature, but are misdirected," and in which the characters "are devoid of truthfulness, are not in harmony with the actual world, and have, therefore, but little more power to move our sympathies than the romances of the middle ages, or the ghost stories which made our granddames tremble."[9]

Sydney Dobell is usually given credit for writing the first complete appreciation of the book, in an article appearing in the *Palladium* shortly before the publication of the second edition. True, Dobell expatiated on the brilliance of the work more fully than had anyone else, and he rhapsodized in glowing rhetoric: "One looks back at the whole story as to a world of brilliant figures in an atmosphere of mist; shapes that come out upon the eye, and burn their colours into the brain, and depart into the enveloping fog." But he makes the gross error of failing to perceive that it is the mature work of a sensitive artist. It is, he says, "the unformed writing of a giant's hand: the 'large utterance' of a baby god." He assumes that *Wuthering Heights* is the first product of the mind that produced *Wildfell Hall*, *Jane Eyre*, and *Shirley*—in that order. Finally, he is confident that

she will not let her next dark-haired hero babble away the respect of her reader and the awe of his antecedents; nor will she find another housekeeper who remembers two volumes *literatim*. . . . She will not, again, employ her wonderful pencil on a picture so destitute of moral beauty and human worth.[10]

Charlotte, eagerly seeking for any sign of a break in public opinion, pounced on Dobell's article with enthusiasm; we today find our enthusiasm tempered by scepticism.

The thirty years between the essays by Dobell and Swin-

[9] *Athenaeum*, XXIII (1850), 1368–1369; *Eclectic Review*, XCIII (1851), 222-227.
[10] "Currer Bell," *Palladium*, September, 1850. Reprinted in *Life and Letters of Sydney Dobell*, ed. E. Jolly (London, 1878), I, 163–186.

burne (the latter considered by some literary historians to be epochmaking in its attitude towards *Wuthering Heights*), though not the desert it was once considered, brought forth a few bushes which are essentially only variations on the established species. The praise is rhapsodic rather than analytical; the faults usurp the foreground and are presented in the most unequivocal language. John Skelton illustrates the rhapsodic tendency. Speaking of the hero of *Wuthering Heights* as compared with Charlotte's, he writes:

> In Emily's we are conscious of something more. A volcano is beneath the flowers where we stand, and we cannot tell where it may burst. There is a refrain of fierce poetry in the men and women she draws—gleams of the gipsy savageness and of the gipsy tenderness. . . . They flutter on the confines between our love and our hate. Their caprice, their sullenness, their mercilessness, hurt and revolt us; but we cannot abandon them to perdition without a prayer that they may be saved.

Or consider this comment:

> "Wuthering Heights" . . . shows a massive strength which is of the rarest description. Its power is absolutely Titanic: from the first page to the last it reads like the intellectual throes of a giant. It is fearful, it is true, and perhaps one of the most unpleasant books ever written. . . . In Heathcliff, Emily Brontë has drawn the greatest villain extant, after Iago. He has no match out of Shakespeare.

Such appreciation reaches its nadir with W. W. Kinsley's judgment: " 'Wuthering Heights' is, therefore, regarded by me with exceptional interest, not because of any artistic worth, but because, despite all its imperfections, it serves to body forth the superb soul of Emily Brontë."[11] Considering the vast amount

---

[11] John Skelton, "Charlotte Brontë," in *Essays in History and Biography* (Edinburgh, 1883), p. 304 (first published in 1857); George B. Smith, "The Brontës," in *Poets and Novelists* (London, 1875), p. 239 (first published in the *Cornhill Magazine*, XXVIII, 1873); and W. W. Kinsley, *The Brontë Sisters* (London, 1899), p. 40 (first published in *Views on Vexed Questions*, 1881). For comments similar to these see also "The Life and Writings of Emily Brontë," *Galaxy*, XV (1873), 234; and T. Wemyss Reid, *Charlotte Brontë* (New York, 1877), pp. 209–210.

of rhapsodical nonsense scattered throughout all these essays, the one attempt at analysis, however slight and incorrect, strikes one forcibly. Heathcliff's character is analysed thus :

> No redeeming, that is, no really human trait lightens the black night of Heathcliff's character. From first to last he manifests to all, save the elder Catherine, that ferocity and faithlessness which a gypsy, according to the strange law of his race, is bound to maintain to all save his own people. . . . Heathcliff's conduct proceeds in a great measure from the entire absorption of all his faculties in one idea; but even admitting that view of the case, he is not human, and not being human he is not real.

And at the same time that this writer condemns the main characters of the book, he defends the author against charges that had been made earlier :

> No amount of sophistry would persuade anyone that Heathcliff was a noble nature, warped by adverse circumstances; or that the elder Catherine was anything but fierce, faithless, and foolish. . . . [But] though a brutal, it is not a sensual book; though coarse, it is not vulgar; though bad, it is not indecent.[12]

Such criticism is at least saner than that of Kinsley, who concludes that "Heathcliff is unquestionably insane," that "a mental and moral madness followed the glare and shock of that falling thunder-bolt" of Catherine's giving him up for Linton.[13]

Tours de force born of desperation in a critical give and take are achieved by Peter Bayne and T. Wemyss Reid. Neither of them, obviously, could stomach the red meat of *Wuthering Heights*—they were both, I am convinced, literary vegetarians; yet they knew that such fare furnishes strength obtainable in no other manner. Hence they condemn but condone, refusing to swallow, but enjoying the taste. The result is acute literary indigestion :

> It were a strange and surely a distempered criticism which hesitated to

---

[12] *Galaxy*, XV (1873), 233, 229.   [13] Kinsley, *op. cit.*, pp. 19, 20.

pass sentence of condemnation on *Wuthering Heights*. . . . Canons of art sound and imperative, true tastes and natural instincts, of which these canons are the expressions, unite in pronouncing it unquestionable and irremediably monstrous. . . . Yet we have perfect confidence in pointing to *Wuthering Heights*, as a work containing evidence of powers it were perhaps impossible to estimate, and mental wealth which we might vainly attempt to compute. . . . In the case both of Cathy and Heathcliff, there was unquestionably a degree of [madness]. But the defence can at best be partial, for, we submit, bedlam is no legitimate sphere of art. . . . The girl's hand which drew Heathcliff and Cathy, which never shook as it brought out those lines of agony on cheek and brow, which never for a moment lost its strength and sweep, flourish or bravura, was such as has seldom wielded either pen or pencil.

T. Wemyss Reid is scarcely better. His attempt to reconcile the seeming irreconcilable opposites of Emily's genius and her devilish book outdoes Sydney Dobell's effort:

It is true that as a novel it is repulsive and almost ghastly. As one reads chapter after chapter of the horrible chronicles of Heathcliff's crimes, the only literary work that can be recalled for comparison with it is the gory tragedy of "Titus Andronicus." From the first page to the last there is hardly a redeeming feature in the book. . . . The hero himself is the most unmitigated villain in fiction; and there is hardly a personage in the story who is not in some shape or another the victim of mental or moral deformities. Nobody can pretend that such a story as this ever ought to have been written; nobody can read it without feeling that its author must herself have had a morbid if not a diseased mind. [But he continues:] When a woman has lived such a life as that of "Ellis Bell," her first literary effort must be regarded as the attempt of an innocent and ignorant child. . . . "Wuthering Heights," then, is the work of one who, in everything but years, was a mere child, and its great and glaring faults are to be forgiven as one forgives the mistakes of childhood. But how vast was the intellectual greatness displayed in this juvenile work! . . . Surely nowhere in modern English fiction can more striking proof be found of the possession of "the creative gift" in an extraordinary degree than is to be obtained in "Wuthering Heights."[14]

---

[14] Peter Bayne, "Ellis, Acton, and Currer Bell," in *Essays in Biography and Criticism*, First Series (Boston, 1857), pp. 398–402; and Reid, *op. cit.*, pp. 202, 204. This argument of uncontrolled genius warbling its native woodnotes wild appears more than once in Brontë criticism. It is reminiscent somehow of one early attitude towards Shakespeare.

Swinburne has usually been given credit for inaugurating a new period in Brontë appreciation; yet if one studies his essay, inspired by the appearance of Mrs. Robinson's biography of Emily, the first full-length study, and formed as a kind of review article of it, one concludes that though he *might* have written the first good analysis of *Wuthering Heights*, he didn't. Mrs. Robinson, so far as she concerned herself with the book as a work of art, seemed primarily interested in the inspiration of the novel; but she insists rightly that Heathcliff is the central figure and that he harms no one seriously who had not either harmed him or asked for trouble and that his punishment is the wrecking of his own life and a lifelong torment. Swinburne insists on the inevitability of the story, its tragic quality (because Emily's whole genius was essentially tragic), and the "high and healthy" quality of the pervading atmosphere; and he defends the book against the charge of awkward construction brought on by its indirect method of narration; but he concerns himself not at all with such questions as why the novel is a tragedy, what Emily Brontë was trying to do and say, why *Wuthering Heights* is the masterpiece that he insists it is. Then, too, though he defends its construction, he admits that it is not only different and difficult, but awkward. Swinburne was by no means the first to sense the overpowering greatness of the book, and he did little more than his predecessors to help us understand the reasons for its greatness.[15]

Before the end of the nineteenth century the Brontë Society was founded and Brontë scholarship became increasingly voluminous, but these efforts did little at first to increase our understanding of *Wuthering Heights* as a work of art.[16] The Vic-

---

[15] See A. Mary F. Robinson [Duclaux], *Emily Brontë* (Boston, 1883), esp. pp. 209, 221; and A. C. Swinburne, "Emily Brontë," in *Miscellanies*, 2nd ed. (London, 1895), pp. 260–270 (first appeared in the *Athenaeum* for 1883).

[16] For the past forty years, however, many of the best discussions of Emily and her novel have been given as addresses before this Society.

torians, still in the saddle, handled this monstrosity in their
stride. Mrs. Oliphant in her literary history gives Emily one
sentence: "Emily Brontë, the second sister . . . , a person of so
much character and force that her personality was almost violent, wrote one wild story, 'Wuthering Heights,' full of fierce
life and tragedy, and the breath of moorland winds and storms,
and several short poems of a remarkable character, died, having
fought out her short life, beating her wings like an imprisoned
bird against the bars of her cage."[17] Leslie Stephen in the influ-
ential *DNB* judges her not worthy of a separate entry, but mentions *Wuthering Heights* in his discussion of Charlotte: "The
novel missed popularity by general painfulness of situation, by
clumsiness of construction, and by absence of the astonishing
power of realisation manifest in 'Jane Eyre.' In point of style it
is superior, but it is the nightmare of a recluse, not a direct
representation of facts seen by a genius." Nor did Frederick
Harrison deem her of any greater importance: "In considering
the gifted Brontë family, it is really Charlotte alone who finally
concerns us. Emily Brontë was a wild, original, and striking
creature, but her one book is a kind of prose *Kubla Khan*—a
nightmare of the superheated imagination."[18] It is at the close
of these decades, too, that *Wuthering Heights* is first admitted
into a history of the novel. W. L. Cross is also, surprisingly
enough, the first—but not the last—critic to link this work with
the Gothic tradition: "The long vista of the purely Gothic
romance . . . is closed by a storm and passion beaten house on
the Yorkshire moors. . . . Beyond the madness and terror of
'Wuthering Heights,' romantic fiction has never gone."[19]

[17] *The Victorian Age in English Literature* (New York, 1892), I, 305.
[18] "Charlotte Brontë," in *Studies in Early Victorian Literature* (London, 1895),
p. 161. The amazing attitude towards Coleridge is worth notice. See also Leslie
Stephen's strictures in his essay, "Charlotte Brontë," in *Hours in a Library* (London,
1892), III, 1–30, esp. p. 27.
[19] *The Development of the English Novel* (New York, 1899), pp. 166–167.

Authorship and sources are treated lengthily by Francis Leyland, who in his attempt to rehabilitate Branwell credited the
novel to him, and William Wright, who traced the inspiration
for *Wuthering Heights* back to Irish experiences of Patrick
Brontë's pseudo-forebears. Both ghosts have finally been laid.[20]

Though much of the other criticism during these years was
equally beside the mark, not all of it was so hopeless as this.
Saintsbury, it is true, speaking before the Brontë Society in its
youthful days, straddles the fence in time-honoured manner:

> In *Wuthering Heights* itself the actual combination of the normal and
> the abnormal, of realism and transcendentalism, is shewn perhaps more
> strikingly than anywhere else. . . . But Emily Brontë was, after all, rather
> a poet than a novelist, and in this book . . . it would be unreasonable to
> expect perfection of the method or indication of its general applicableness.
> Despite the intense reality of much of the scenery and of such characters
> as Joseph and the elder Catherine, the thing is on the whole rather un-
> earthly; the never explained origin of Heathcliff and some other points
> leave it too close upon the confines of the fairy tales, and there are many
> other technical drawbacks.[21]

Arthur Colton, however, defends her strongly against the
charge of monstrosity of characters, for "*Goneril* and *Regan* are
certainly as monstrous as *Heathcliff*," who is as probable as
Dickens's Daniel Quilp or Massinger's Sir Giles Overreach. Nor
will he admit that the atmosphere is "ghoulish," but rather
"more in the manner of Marlowe's 'Jew of Malta,' or Webster's
'Vittoria Corombona,' particularly the latter." "J.F.," though
more eulogistic than analytical, stresses the uniqueness of the

---

[20] F. A. Leyland, *The Brontë Family* (London, 1886); and William Wright, *The
Brontës in Ireland* (London, 1893). A. M. Mackay, in *The Brontës: Fact and Fiction*
(London, 1897), demolished Wright's argument; the Branwell legend persisted to quite
recent times.

[21] "The Position of the Brontës as Origins in the History of the English Novel,"
Transactions of the Brontë Society, II (1906), 26 (address delivered in 1899). Years later,
in his study of the English novel (1913), he disposed of the book in fewer words:
"Emily's work, *Wuthering Heights*, is one of those isolated books, which, whatever
their merit, are rather ornaments than essential parts in novel history" (p. 243).

work and the "transcendent genius" that produced it; and an anonymous writer in the *Atlantic Monthly* blurts out part of the true reason the novel had not been correctly evaluated and winds up with some wishful thinking:

> The reader of to-day, indeed, appreciates it far more truly than any reader of its own epoch did, or could have done. . . . The book was curiously and, so far as its author was concerned, distressingly in advance of its time. . . . The utmost which this grim tale found, for years, at the hands even of its most merciful critics was apology; then a generation arose for which it possessed a sort of fearful fascination; and now, at last, it commands a cult, and is acknowledged to have founded a school.[22]

Arthur Salmon, on the other hand, introduced a new motif, one which was to have disastrous consequences in our own century. With him the autobiographical school of interpretation was implied, if not explicitly stated:

> For a solitary girl to have invented such scenes and such language would have been impossible; but with Emily Brontë they are merely transcripts from life. There had been an archetype for it all at Haworth; and the girl's experience was almost entirely limited to her home. She painted the life she knew; it was her misfortune, not her fault, that this life contained such terrible scenes. . . . It might not be altogether a good sign for such works to be popular; they are for a "fit audience, though few,"—not for the many. . . . Not every reader can assimilate such strong food, or turn it to good purpose. . . . Faulty as a narrative, "Wuthering Heights" burns with energy and pulses with life-blood.[23]

The depth to which such criticism could descend is shown clearly in two works published during the first two decades of

---

[22] Arthur W. Colton, "Emily Brontë," *Citizen*, II (1896), 12; J. F., "*Wuthering Heights*," *Temple Bar*, LXXXI (1887), 568; "Girl Novelists of the Time," *Atlantic Monthly*, LX (1887), 707. Note also Clement Shorter's comments in *Charlotte Brontë and Her Circle* (London, 1896), pp. 158–159, with his emphasis on the inspiration of the book; and A. M. Williams, "Emily Brontë," *Temple Bar*, XCVIII (1893), 431–439, with his insistence on the fine delineation of character and the beauty of certain passages of the book.
[23] "A Modern Stoic: Emily Brontë," *Poet-Lore*, IV (1892), 66, 70.

this century. John Malham-Dembleby "proves" that Charlotte wrote *Wuthering Heights* and was the heroine to M. Heger's hero in all the Brontë novels. All the principal characters are identified with real people, and the books become then merely a kind of diary of Charlotte's love life. But Mrs. Chadwick's study, though less bold and egotistical, is scarcely better, since she reads *Wuthering Heights* only for the light it throws on biography and concludes also with a well-established set of identifications between the fictional characters and such people as M. Heger and Charlotte and Patrick Brontë.[24]

Yet some years before Malham-Dembleby and Mrs. Chadwick capitalized on the popularity of the Brontë legend, an address before the Brontë Society produced what is basically the first competent attempt at analysis of the book. James Fotheringham was by no means radical in his solution of the problem of construction; he was not nearly so rhapsodic in his praise as Swinburne had been; but he makes a brief, and reasonably satisfactory, analysis of the philosophical achievement of the novel and of what Emily was trying to do. Of the first he says: "Not only is the book strong but the drift and moral of the book *please*, please that is in the high sense,—they satisfy our higher feelings and principles, and please as the severe order of the world pleases when we have caught its issues." And of the second he concludes: "It is a study of the development and issues of evil, of anti-social passions, of hate and malice, working freely, backed and unfolded by exceptional strength and ability." In analysing Heathcliff further, Fotheringham finds that "the elements and evolution of *Wuthering Heights* are fairly set on laws of the soul, within the moral sphere," that Heathcliff's problem is in part the same as Edmund's in *King*

[24] John Malham-Dembleby, *The Key to the Brontë Works* (London: Walter Scott, 1911); and Mrs. Ellis H. Chadwick, *In the Footsteps of the Brontës* (London: Sir I. Pitman, 1914), pp. 321–354. The first reminds one inevitably of the Baconian heresy.

Lear, that though Heathcliff has no morality through the larger part of the story, yet even such natures are held by morality and have eventually to answer for themselves, if not for the world, certain questions about the end and good of their actions. Finally, though this is not a detailed study of the artistry of the novel, some aspects such as the conclusion are dealt with.

> The close of the book seems to show on the author's part a sense of how exactly yet how genially in the great course of the years Nature takes her own laws, how the errors are adjusted, the wrongs healed, the tragedy of men's egoisms buried in peace, while about all the trouble of life and outlasting it all is Nature's own quiet greatness and beauty.[25]

The course of Brontë criticism, however, was not materially altered by this analysis. *Wuthering Heights*, for example, was noticed at greater length, but still sketchily, by most literary historians; but the appraisals continued to show the same split personality. Dawson indulges in panegyric for more than two pages without making any sound critical judgments; Nicoll and Seccombe ally it with the Radcliffe, Fouqué, or Hoffmann schools; Burton disposes of the entire problem in a page (the Brontë sisters had no influence because they came at the wrong time); Walker admits its power but also its unpleasantness; Phelps calls it "more hysterical than historical in its treatment of human nature"; Miss Whitmore feels that Heathcliff is only repulsive and that Catherine is the centre of the story; Jack makes the oft-heard comparison between *Wuthering Heights* and *Jane Eyre*; Williams finds it a "transcript of her own mind, temperament, and soul."[26] All of these are no more than repetitions or variants of old themes.

---

[25] James Fotheringham, "The Work of Emily Brontë and the Brontë Problem," *Transactions of the Brontë Society*, II (1906), 116, 118, 126–127, 128. The paper was read to the Society in 1900.

[26] W. J. Dawson, *The Makers of English Fiction* (New York: Revell, 1905), pp. 141–142; W. R. Nicoll and Thomas Seccombe, *A History of English Literature* (New York: Dodd, Mead, 1907), p. 1166; Richard Burton, *Masters of the English Novel*

In separate essays, too, the same equivocation, the same contradictory statements continue to appear. William Dean Howells emphasizes once again the awkward structure ("seldom has a great romance been worse contrived"); J. B. Henneman classes much of the book as "fantastical nonsense," but finds mingled with this "pages writ deep in human misery and life"; Mary E. Wilkins combines "repulsive" and "power" in time-honoured fashion ('it has the repulsiveness of power"); Mrs. Humphrey Ward floats the novel on the stream of the European romantic movement and finds its fountainhead in the German romantic imagination; H. M. Allen contrasts the external inspiration which produced Charlotte's novels with the "subjective analysis" which went into *Wuthering Heights*. This last, especially, makes a series of inept comparisons:

> Emily comes closer to Edgar Allan Pope [*sic*] in temperament, conception, and spontaneity of utterance than any other who has ever written. Here and there will be found a suggestion of Thomas Hardy or, again, of Coleridge, but the prevailing power in her work is the wild, mystic spirit that pervades "The Fall of the House of Usher."[27]

Amid such criticism it is with almost a sense of relief that one discovers a writer who doesn't like the book and says so. Such a man is W. F. Lord, who dogmatically asserts that "Ellis Bell was not a great artist," that even *Agnes Grey* is better than *Wuthering Heights,* and who continues:

(New York: Holt, 1909), p. 259; Hugh Walker, *The Literature of the Victorian Era* (Cambridge University Press, 1910), p. 723; W. L. Phelps, *The Advance of the English Novel* (New York: Dodd, Mead, 1916), p. 118; Clara H. Whitmore, *Woman's Work in English Fiction* (New York: Putnam, 1910), p. 252; A. A. Jack, "The Brontës," in *CHEL*, XIII, 455–456; Harold Williams, *Two Centuries of the English Novel* (London: Smith, Elder, 1911), pp. 220–221.

[27] See W. D. Howells, "The Two Catherines of Emily Brontë," in *Heroines of Fiction* (New York: Harpers, 1901), I, 230; J. B. Henneman, "The Brontë Sisters," *Sewanee Review*, IX (1901), 231; Mary E. Wilkins, "Emily Brontë and 'Wuthering Heights,' " *Booklovers Magazine*, I (1903), 514; Mrs. Humphrey Ward, "Wuthering Heights," *Transactions of the Brontë Society*, II (1906), 227–232; H. M. Allen, "Emily Brontë–One Hundred Years After," *Education*, XXXIX (1918), 228.

The school of thought which lays it down that form is essential, that perfection should be aimed at, that slovenliness and disregard of authority is a blemish in otherwise sound work, that maintains that reverence is due to all thought and to all work whether remunerative or not—this school still lives, if it languishes, in one great seat of learning; and this is the school to which the Brontë influence, whether for good or for ill, is antagonistic.[28]

To balance this first completely dissident voice in some years, we reap the usual crop of panegyrists, including this time such forceful voices as those of Maurice Maeterlinck and Virginia Woolf, who, no matter how rhapsodic their praise, help us little in understanding the book. To this group must be added M. Dimnet, for whom the "least original and the only perishable part of her talent" is the simple romanticism of "Heathcliff the demon," but who seizes upon the "dominant sexuality which pervades the whole book" as Emily's great gift to literature. Only C. E. Vaughan attempts analysis, and he is primarily interested in the sisters rather than their creations.[29]

Since 1920, more rational, sensible criticism on *Wuthering Heights* has appeared than during the seventy-odd preceding years, criticism aimed at analysing various technical aspects of the book and in at least one essay synthesizing the answers into a well-integrated study. Yet the same years have seen well-nigh meaningless rhapsodies, recurrent remarks on construction, struggles over the authorship, new twists in comparison, and autobiographical interpretations, partly under the influence of Freudian psychology.

The rhapsodic effusions doubtless evidence a personal interest

[28] "The Brontë Novels," *Nineteenth Century and After*, LIII (1903), 484, 495.

[29] See Maurice Maeterlinck, *Wisdom and Destiny*, tr. Alfred Sutro (New York: Dodd, Mead, 1910), pp. 302–303, 311–312; Virginia Woolf, " ' Jane Eyre' and 'Wuthering Heights,' " *The Common Reader* (London: L. and V. Woolf, 1925), pp. 196–204 (essay written in 1916); Ernest Dimnet, *The Brontë Sisters*, tr. L. M. Sill (London: Cape, 1927), p. 172 (originally published in 1910); and C. E. Vaughan, "Charlotte and Emily Brontë: A Comparison and Contrast," *Transactions of the Brontë Society*, IV (1912), 217–235.

in the book and a sense of its power, but they ask no questions about its status as a work of art. Thus W. B. White remarks:

> Probably, however, the greatness of the book lies mainly in the extraordinary love between Cathy and Heathcliff, and in the way the mystical effect of that love gives atmosphere throughout. Emily's knowledge of love is deep and wonderful: she had plumbed the depths and scaled the heights of the divine passion.

And F. A. Bullock:

> In her book you have it all—the cry for integration and wholeness. Humanity dies without nature; nature, evil and unsatisfied, without humanity. She saw, she felt, she knew the loneliness, the guilt, and redemption of that twin, but divided, reality—Nature and Humanity. If we can in any degree understand by feeling what she saw and said, then we shall know that her genius has brought vision to our imagination and the healing of peace to our divided souls.[30]

A bare mention is sufficient for those writers who continue to harp on the poor construction of the novel. Oliver Elton, Arthur Symons, Miss Bald, and H. W. Garrod—all emphasize in one way or another the dishevelled quality of the structure.[31] Norman Collins objects to the way the tale "leaps from narrative to narrative like a frog, and flashes across the generations like a dragon fly"; Lovett and Hughes insist that the story is "clumsily introduced and told by an illiterate servant, in a style which is Emily Brontë's own"; Pelham Edgar mentions two technical flaws (but, he admits, the book overrides them): having Ellen Dean strain convention by her knowledge of certain facts, and

---

[30] W. B. White, *The Miracle of Haworth* (Univ. of London Press, 1937), p. 230; and F. A. Bullock, "The Genius of Emily Brontë," *Transactions of the Brontë Society*, IX (1940), 128 (address delivered to the Society in 1937). See also G. F. Bradby, "Emily Brontë," in *The Brontës and Other Essays* (London: Oxford, 1932), p. 35; and Marjory A. Bald, "The Brontës," in *Women Writers in the Nineteenth Century* (Cambridge University Press, 1923), pp. 97–98.

[31] Oliver Elton, *A Survey of English Literature, 1780–1880* (New York: Macmillan, 1920), IV, 294; Arthur Symons, "Emily Brontë," in *Dramatis Personae* (Indianapolis: Bobbs Merrill, 1923), p. 50; Bald, *op. cit.*, pp. 79, 98–99; H. W. Garrod, ed., *Wuthering Heights* (London: Oxford, 1932), p xiii.

having a break in interest when the elder Cathy dies; E. F. Benson is confused by the relationships between Earnshaws, Lintons, and Heathcliffs, which "would baffle a professional genealogist."[32]

The old question of authorship continues to plague us, but not with the eager insistence of Leyland and Malham-Dembleby. E. F. Benson concludes that Branwell must have written the first two chapters and been in on all of it; Miss Willis and Miss Ratchford deny him any part in authorship; and W. B. White, while agreeing with the ladies, admits his influence as a model. Even E. A. Baker is willing to concede the opening part to Branwell. Finally, in her fictionalized biography, Dorothy Cornish gives the final turn of the screw by having Branwell tell Emily the story, which Emily then writes in her own way.[33] The trail blazed by Dr. Wright in the nineteenth century concerning the sources of the story is followed by Florence Dry as she attempts to prove that Scott's *Black Dwarf* was used as a base for the setting, characters, and plot of *Wuthering Heights*, and Romer Wilson as she insists that "the framework of *this story of an Entail* was borrowed outright from *The Entail* by E. T. W. Hoffmann."[34]

New trails, too, are blazed in the matter of literary comparisons. In the preceding century Emily Brontë and her novel had

[32] Norman Collins, *The Facts of Fiction* (London: Gollancz, 1932), p. 186; R. M. Lovett and H. S. Hughes, *The History of the Novel in England* (Boston: Houghton Mifflin, 1932), p. 284; Pelham Edgar, *The Art of the Novel* (New York: Macmillan, 1933), pp. 144–145; E. F. Benson, "The Brontës," in *The English Novelists*, ed. by Derek Verschoyle (New York: Harcourt, Brace, 1936), p. 168.

[33] E. F. Benson, *Charlotte Brontë* (London: Longmans, 1932), pp. 168–179; Irene C. Willis, *The Authorship of Wuthering Heights* (London: Hogarth, 1936); F. E. Ratchford, *The Brontës' Web of Childhood* (New York: Columbia University Press), p. 247; White, *op. cit.*, pp. 223–242; E. A. Baker, *The History of the English Novel* (London: H. F. & G. Witherby, 1937), VIII, 76; Dorothy H. Cornish, *These Were the Brontës* (New York: Macmillan, 1940), pp. 390 ff.

[34] Florence S. Dry, *The Sources of "Wuthering Heights"* (Cambridge: Heffer, 1937); and Romer Wilson, *The Life and Private History of Emily Jane Brontë* (New York: Boni, 1928), p. 246.

been compared most often to Elizabethan dramatists and their tragedies, especially Shakespeare's and Webster's. These two comparisons still appear, and the relationship between *Wuthering Heights* and the tales of terror is still insisted upon;[35] but new, more contemporary parallels are also drawn. Balzac, Dostoyevski, and Germanic myth are now coupled up with Brontë for the first time. According to Prince Mirsky, the novel combines the qualities of "spiritual intensity and artistic efficiency" as no other novel does, with the possible exception of *Crime and Punishment*; and Benson notes that "Catherine, like Brynhilde, mates with a mortal, but she is not mortal herself. . . . Anyone who attempts to criticize *Wuthering Heights* must do so from this transcendental standpoint." But perhaps the most startling equation is that by Weygandt:

It is not the characters of the story that are the best of it, but the passion with which it is imagined and the passion with which it is told, a passion that raises certain passages of it to a lyric abandon that had not been in the novel before she and her sister Charlotte had written. You must turn to the great passages of lyric prose that distinguish the essay to find parallels, to Sir Thomas Browne, to Carlyle and to Emerson.[36]

The autobiographical school of critics has reacted in various ways, some as usual being contradictory to others. Keighley Snowden, for example, contends that the passion shown in the novel is the result of the love Emily felt for the curate Weightman: "*Wuthering Heights* is, I do not hesitate to say, the masterpiece of one who had lived through a dire experience of passion and overwhelming doubt, but who had overridden both and put them behind her." On the other hand, Alexander Woollcott (even he spoke his piece!) insists that it is "less the

---

[35] See, for example, Symons, *op. cit.*, p. 50; Baker, *op. cit.*, VIII, 69; Edith Birkhead, *The Tale of Terror* (London: Constable, 1921), pp. 224–225; and Garrod, ed., *Wuthering Heights*, p. xiii.

[36] Prince D. S. Mirsky, "Emily Brontë," *London Mercury*, VII (1923), 272; Benson, "The Brontës," p. 168–169; Cornelius Weygandt, *A Century of the English Novel* (New York: Century, 1925), p. 105. See also Baker, *op. cit.*, VIII, 69.

E

result of an amorous experience than a substitute for one. . . .
When I think of *Wuthering Heights*, I prefer to chip off a bit
from an immortal fragment and describe that novel as the cry
of 'woman wailing for her demon-lover.' "[37] But these are in-
nocuous compared to the two full-length studies in which Freudian psychology runs rampant. In both (one the product of
England, the other of America), *Wuthering Heights* is read as
pure autobiography in which Emily is not only Heathcliff, but
Catherine too, and even a little of Ellen Dean. For Romer
Wilson,

consciousness came to Emily in the form of Heathcliff, a dark waif of no
clime, or country, or parentage. From the moment he came she began to
lead a double life, his life, and the life of Catherine. . . . At Catherine's
death in *Wuthering Heights*, the autobiography comes to an end. Then
Emily did a curious thing, she re-wrote the story as it might have been
without Heathcliff as hero.

But for Virginia Moore the matter is not even so simple as this.
The book, and the poetry as well, grew out of one crucial experience of her life, either a Lesbian love affair or love for a
so-called Louis Parensell.

Wuthering Heights is a tremendous allegory, by the writing of which
Emily shrived herself of her "sin" as a penitent bathes in icy water at the
hour of death. . . . For Emily, in the scheme of correspondences in this
allegory that is autobiography, is, without a shadow of doubt, Heathcliff.
But since a personality is multiple and . . . a novelist often splits his
personality to form not one but several characters, Emily in her superficial
and acquired aspects partakes a little of the nature of Cathy and even Ellen
Dean.[38]

Criticism, in my opinion, can become no wilder than this!

---

[37] Keighley Snowden, "The Enigma of Emily Brontë," *Fortnightly Review*, CXXX
(1928), 200, 202; and Alexander Woollcott, " 'Our Greatest Woman,' or Screen Credit
for Emily," in *Long, Long Ago* (New York: Viking, 1943), pp. 213–214 (originally
published in the *Ladies' Home Journal*, June, 1939).
[38] See Romer Wilson, *op. cit., passim*, esp. pp. 261, 263; and Virginia Moore, *The
Life and Eager Death of Emily Brontë* (London: Rich and Cowan, 1936), pp. 320 ff.

Most, but not quite all, of the remaining essays and studies are commendable. Two writers, for example, try to deal seriously with certain problems, but their conclusions scarcely seem valid. H. W. Garrod suggests that Mr. Lockwood, far from being a mere excrescence, was for Emily Brontë the most necessary person in the cast. She meant to make *Wuthering Heights* a novel of edification about primeval love in order to improve Mr. Lockwood, who, modern, elegant, and sophisticated, knows only the urban attitude towards love. Richard Chase, in the most recent essay to come to my attention, deals with the material and the central themes of the Brontë fiction. The materials came from the social customs of the day, and the writers rebelled against these customs "only in the sense that they transmuted the Victorian social situation into mythical and symbolic forms." The central theme of all these novels is the manner in which the sexual and intellectual energy of the male is brought under control by women.[39] Brilliant light is thrown on the relation between *Wuthering Heights* and the Gondal poems, those cloudy romances of adolescence and early maturity, by Leicester Bradner and especially by Miss Ratchford, whose studies enable us to project the masterpiece against the literary background from which it developed.[40] Mr. Ralli examines the novel for the light it throws on Emily's personality. Herbert Read, though primarily concerned with the qualities of art and personality in the Bontë sisters, concludes on an admirable note: " 'Wuthering Heights,' with its unerring unity of conception and its full catharsis of the emotions of pity and terror, is one of the very few occasions on which the novel has

---

[39] Garrod, ed., *Wuthering Heights*, pp. viii–ix; and Richard Chase, "The Brontës: A Centennial Observance," *Kenyon Review*, IX (1947), 487–506.

[40] Leicester Bradner, "The Growth of 'Wuthering Heights,' " *PMLA*, XLVIII (1933), 129–146; and F. E. Ratchford, *op. cit.*, *passim*, especially pp. 240–247. Mr. Bradner also considers Hoffmann's "The Entail" and "The Bridegroom of Barna," a story published in *Blackwood's* (1840), as contributing influences, but not sources.

reached the dignity of classical tragedy." And E. M. Forster is equally admirable in his comment on one technical aspect—the reconcilement of the "muddle, chaos, tempest" with the elaborately accurate time chart of the novel.[41] But it is primarily four studies in this period which have made the greatest contribution to our understanding of the book as a work of art.

C. P. Sanger's *The Structure of Wuthering Heights* deals entirely with technical aspects of the novel, but it is vital for our understanding of the maturity of legal knowledge shown therein and the care with which the chronology was planned. Although on the surface the time element is chaotic and confused, every major event can be accurately dated. Its total effect, its coherence and unity, its form, and its presiding significance are what Lascelles Abercrombie is intent on showing.

> The book enlarges the nature of tragedy : it shows how a genuinely tragic action can be carried on past the fatality into an ending in positive happiness. . . . At the cost of some very superficial and very excusable clumsiness, Emily succeeded in compacting her turbulent and explosive matter into lucidly shapely form; and by that means the whole book becomes the expression of one central and dominant motive. The rarest achievement in the art of the novel seems to be absolute here : "Wuthering Heights" has that perfect coherence of purpose we think of when we think of the art of Shakespeare's tragedy or Beethoven's symphony.

An analysis of Heathcliff's character is the main purpose of J. A. Mackereth in his Brontë Society address. Concerning the environmental influence on Heathcliff's behaviour, his position at the centre of the book, the different stages in his development, and his love for Cathy, Mackereth is excellent.[42]

---

[41] Augustus Ralli, "Emily Brontë: The Problem of Personality," *North American Review*, CCXXI (1925), 495–507; Herbert Read, "Charlotte and Emily Brontë," *Yale Review*, XIV (1925), 738; and E. M. Forster, *Aspects of the Novel* (New York : Harcourt, Brace, 1927), p. 210.

[42] C. P. Sanger, *The Structure of Wuthering Heights* (London : L. and V. Woolf, 1926); Lascelles Abercrombie, "The Brontës To-day," *Transactions of the Brontë Society*, VI (1925), pp. 196–199; and James A. Mackereth, "The Greatness of Emily Brontë," *Transactions of the Brontë Society*, VII (1931), 175–200.

The most complete, thorough, and penetrating analysis and interpretation of *Wuthering Heights* to date, however, is the work of Lord David Cecil. Though perhaps too much weight is put on the metaphysical quality of the novel, Lord David has with eminent sanity come to grips with most, if not all, of the artistic and structural problems which must be solved for an understanding of any work of art. For him, the setting is a microcosm of the universal scheme as Emily Brontë conceived it, and the theme is the destruction and re-establishment of cosmic harmony. That she was writing a philosophical, cosmic drama, I am not sure; but Lord David's analysis makes sense— as many other comments on the novel do not. It is well bolstered with references to the novel itself; and it takes into account various aspects of character, plot, setting, and style.[43]

Never, probably, will an interpretation of *Wuthering Heights* be made which will satisfy all people for all time, for a master-piece of art has a life all its own which changes, develops, and unfolds as the generations pass. But the fact that the novel has been read continuously for a hundred years, that even those critics who were most repelled by it felt compelled often to justify their sense of repulsion, that a fit few have in various ways made it easier to understand the book as a work of art, and that after a century such diverse reactions and opinions are still possible gives the comparison of *Wuthering Heights* with Shakespeare's dramas some validity. Like the wuthering heights themselves, it has withstood the fiercest tempests; it stands sturdy yet, a monument of proof that a work of art can be strengthened by the sunny breezes of favourable criticism, but cannot be destroyed by critical storms.

---

[43] *Early Victorian Novelists* (Indianapolis: Bobbs, Merrill, 1935), pp. 157–203.

Thoughts on
"Wuthering Heights"*

F. H. LANGMAN

WUTHERING HEIGHTS is a novel of genius, with a healthy narrative appeal for undergraduates, and it raises critical problems in an interesting way—all of which makes it an excellent choice to set in undergraduate English courses. But a problem then comes up. What critics should we recommend? Or, failing that, what critics will students in any event turn to? Too much of the published criticism is badly written, critically evasive, and (sometimes) just inaccurate. I'm raising the matter in the form in which it presents itself to me, but I think it will have some interest for others concerned with literary criticism. It may be useful at least to nail down some common faults in the criticism of this novel, and to point to questions anyone trying seriously to discuss it will have to face.

The main points on which critics fall short are the significance of the prose style and narrative method, the nature of the love between Catherine and Heathcliff, and the pervasive violence and cruelty. On these points critics are prone to lose their heads in a flurry of wild and whirling words, or else to read the book so carelessly that its challenge evaporates in vagueness.

---

* Reprinted by kind permission of the editors from *Essays in Criticism*, Vol. XV (July, 1965).

The problem of style and narrative method is often reduced to complete nonsense. We are told, for example, that "the content is strange enough, indeed baffling enough; while the artistic expression of it is flawless."[1] Or the novel is said to contain "an enigmatic significance which we can never analyse";[2] it is "animated by some mysterious, universal, half-divine life which can only be 'recognized,' not understood."[3]

Similarly the relationship of Catherine and Heathcliff is described as "one of kin rather than of lovers, Heathcliff is a brother in suffering."[4] One ingenious theory makes him literally Catherine's half-brother, a by-blow of one of Earnshaw's previous visits to Liverpool.[5] Their love is "astonishingly ravenous and possessive"[6] (although it is, after all, Edgar who insists upon his possession of Catherine: "Will you give up Heathcliff hereafter, or will you give up me?" Heathcliff's feeling is much more complex: "I never would have banished him from her society as long as she desired his. The moment her regard ceased, I would have torn his heart out"). And yet it is sexless: "The Cathy-Heathcliff relationship is handled in neither sexual nor even particularly human terms."[7] It is, in short, a love so peculiar that it transcends, by definition, all possibility of intelligible discussion: "a wild spiritual affinity between a girl and a boy, both creatures rebelling against the confines of human nature."[8] It "belongs to the realm of the imagination where myths are created."[9]

And so the novel's outlines are dissolved in a universal solvent of mythopoeic criticism:

---

[1] Walter Allen, *The English Novel*.   [2] Edwin Muir, *The Structure of the Novel*.
[3] Dorothy van Ghent, *The English Novel—Form and Function*.
[4] G. D. Klingopulos, "The Novel as Dramatic Poem: *Wuthering Heights*" (*Scrutiny*, XIV, 4).
[5] Eric Solomon, "The Incest Theme in *Wuthering Heights*" (*Nineteenth Century Fiction*, 14, 1).
[6] Van Ghent, *op. cit.*   [7] Boris Ford, *Wuthering Heights* (*Scrutiny*, VII, 4).
[8] Richard Church, *The Growth of the English Novel*.   [9] Van Ghent, *op. cit.*

With a few adjustments to the plot, he [Heathcliff] need not have
entered the story as a human being at all. His part might have been
played by fate, or nature, or God, or the Devil. He is sheer dazzling sexual
and intellectual force.[10]

Once the strategy of this kind of criticism is understood, it is
easy to see how it will sidestep the problem of violence and
cruelty in *Wuthering Heights*. It simply denies that there is any
such problem. Since the characters are not human, moral questions do not apply. In this novel "no conventional morality prevails . . . . here resides a race strangely and abhorrently pro-
tected against the usual consequences of evil deeds."[11] The love
of Catherine and Heathcliff is "perfectly amoral," while Heathcliff himself

is no more ethically relevant than is flood or earthquake or whirlwind . . .
Wuthering Heights so baffles and confounds the ethical sense because it is
not informed with that sense at all.[12]

This sort of comment can only be made in disregard of what
the book contains. By "the ethical sense" is meant, presumably,
an awareness of moral principle as distinct from legal obligation, of the living spirit rather than the dead letter. Now not
only is *Wuthering Heights* informed by an awareness of this
distinction, but Heathcliff of all people is its spokesman :

"That is quite possible . . . quite possible that your master should have
nothing but common humanity and a sense of duty to fall back upon. But
do you imagine that I shall leave Catherine to his *duty* and *humanity*?"

Not all the discussion of this novel proceeds at the level indicated by the passages I've quoted. In turning to criticism which
is more reasonable, which attends to the novel, asks basic ques-

---

[10] Richard Chase, "The Brontës, or, Myth Domesticated" (*Kenyon Review*, IX, 4,
reprinted in *Forms of Modern Fiction*, ed. O'Connor).
[11] Ruth Adams, "*Wuthering Heights*: The Land East of Eden" (*Nineteenth Century Fiction*, 13, 1).
[12] Van Ghent, *op. cit.*

tions, and goes some way to answering them, I shall deal in turn with the main points I raised earlier.

I

On the prose style of *Wuthering Heights*, Mrs. Van Ghent speaks of "an excess everywhere present in language." Mark Schorer makes a stylistic analysis of more subtlety and substance, but he too declares that the novel has an "almost impossibly inflated style."[13] Confronted by such opinions, it seems necessary to say flatly that the novel's style is not uncontrolled, excessive, and unchanging. On the contrary, it combines force and variety with an almost unfaltering control over tone and imagery.

To give substance to these assertions, I shall point to the flexibility and variety of the prose, and the skill with which it is modulated. Consider, for example, the long paragraph on the second page, describing the parlour at the Heights. This paragraph establishes the scene of much of the ensuing action : all the details of furniture are solidly there, and the house is shown to be not unduly rough but well kept and as refined as might be expected of its place and time. The effect is, before the story begins, to anchor it to a reality of time and place, to give it this stable location as distinct from the resonant suggestiveness of the outdoor landscape :

One end . . . reflected splendidly both light and heat from ranks of immense pewter dishes, interspersed with silver jugs and tankards, towering row after row, on a vast oak dresser, to the very roof. The latter had never been underdrawn : its entire anatomy lay bare to an enquiring eye, except where a frame of wood laden with oatcakes and clusters of legs of beef, mutton, and ham, concealed it.

The writing here is precise and methodical (it follows the gaze of the "enquiring eye" up the rows of shining utensils,

---

[13] "Fiction and the 'Analogical Matrix'" (*Kenyon Review*, 1949, reprinted in *Critiques and Essays on Modern Fiction*, ed. Aldridge).

from there along the rafters, then down again along the fire-
place wall), but it is not highly charged. The chief impression
it gives is that it is accurate, dependable. The thorough detail
and workmanlike exposition give an assurance that sanity and
a sense of actuality lie behind the passages of extraordinary
poetic writing for which the novel is usually noted. Poetic intensity may mark the style of the high points : but the strength
of the whole is a prose strength.

The strength of the whole is worth insisting on, because in
concentrating attention upon the love of Catherine and Heathcliff most critics lose too much of the novel's abundant life. Mr.
Klingopulos writes :

> As an Elizabethan play stands or falls by the quality of the poetry at its
> crises of meaning, so *Wuthering Heights* may be said to justify itself by
> the quality of some half-dozen or so speeches of Catherine's and Heath-
> cliff's which are as direct and as highly organized in word and rhythm as
> poetry. In such speeches the novel establishes the reality of its subject
> matter.

The criterion offered here seems unacceptably narrow for
the judgment of an Elizabethan play; applied to a novel it
surely won't do at all. The interest of *Wuthering Heights* may
centre in the passages of most intense emotion, but they possess
their intensity, they convince, only by their place in the whole.
I should say, instead, that the novel convinces us of its reality
—of its being serious and meaningful—by the firmness of its
structure and the integrity of its prose, and that the scenes of
intense emotion can only be understood and judged in relation
to many passages of a quieter strength.

To indicate the nature of that strength I should like to refer
to the passage, too long to quote here, which describes the death
of Mr. Earnshaw. The passage, beginning "But the hour came,
at last, that ended Mr. Earnshaw's troubles," is at the end of
Chapter V.

In this passage, the dramatic effect is beautifully restrained : the surprise is not for the reader, who has been warned by the first sentence, but for the characters only. Attention is thus turned not to the fact that death comes but to the way that it comes. And the nature of the old man's death, as it comes through in the writing, generates a moving and significant symbolism. It is a quiet death, a lapsing out at the completion of a well-lived cycle. In this, it forms a contrast to the premature, painful deaths of Catherine, Hindley, and, later Heathcliff, and to the sterile wasting-away of Edgar. The passage begins with two brief and limpid sentences, rhythmically slow. October—the end of Autumn, the closing of the year. Evening. The orchestrated, subdued suggestions are at work relating human destiny to the universal pattern of closing cycles, gently persuading our minds to accept such a close as inevitable and natural. The third sentence evokes the setting within which death is to be contemplated. It conveys the isolation of humanity within the unliving universe, and hence the mystery of life—isolation, not, while men can draw into community ("we were all together"), loneliness. (Heathcliff and Catherine die essentially alone.) The natural world, brought in by the wind, is heard as "wild and stormy" yet not positively hostile —it is not cold. Within the house, the grouping suggests the inter-relations of the people. The servants are in the same room, not separated from the family yet not quite of it, seated at a remove. Cathy leans against her father's knee, Heathcliff rests his head in her lap. The scene is immensely touching, but without a drop of sentimentality. It is quite clean of the kind of embarrassment we might fear from Dickens in such a place. The calm and peace are inherent in the established regularity of the household under the old man's mastership. At the same time, we are made conscious that the moment of calm is, after all, only momentary. It is one of Cathy's rare moments of quiet-

ness and contrition. In her retort—"Why cannot you always be
a good man, father?"—there is a reminder of her usual nature:
it is subdued here, but not glossed over, not made angelic for the
sake of the scene.

The passage gets much of its strength from its function as a
centre of the organization or pattern of the whole novel, from
the way significances draw together in it and run out again to
make inter-relations with all that follows. The old man's dying
brings to a close a period of stability in the little community
of the Heights. Cathy's moment of recalcitrance is a sign of the
restlessness which will impel the new generation to seek other
satisfactions and to break the discipline of the old settled way
of life. "Restlessness" may be too vague a term. What I mean
is that the generation of Cathy and Heathcliff have become
aware of their energies and emotions in a way unknown to their
elders, and require more developed values than the simple
pieties they have been taught. Cathy's question—"Why cannot
you always be a good man?"—is more than an exhibition of her
pertness. It has a shrewdness, a knowledge that human character is complex and not simply black or white, that her father's
question wholly lacks—"Why canst thou not always be a good
lass, Cathy?"

To describe the novel as a "dramatic poem" is thus unsatisfactory, because it leads to an undervaluing of Emily Brontë's
specific strength as a *novelist*: her command of the wide resources of narrative prose. Another indication of this command
is given by her flexible and organic use of humour. The first
chapters provide a clear illustration. It is important to get the
tone of these chapters right. The weather is the principal means
of creating "atmosphere" in these chapters: by a series of suggestions it sets our expectations in a particular key; it prepares
us for the nightmare with all its implications that follows in
Chapter III, by making us see and feel the premature darkness,

the cold, the isolating, suffocating snow. At the same time a more complex effect is achieved. The tone of the chapters is not wholly grim. The bitterness of the elements presses as a threat behind a lighter, almost farcical element, as Lockwood makes a fool of himself, first at tea and then in his impetuous flight from his boorish hosts. Lockwood's first dream has the same quality, half comedy, half melodrama, which establishes it as an ordinary nightmare to set off the poignant reality of the second dream.

In Cathy's diary the comic note is different. Like her drawing of Joseph, her description of his sermon evinces a quality often overlooked in assessments of her personality. She is one of the few characters with a sense of humour. Moreover it is not of the frivolous facetious sort displayed by Lockwood. A genuine comic verve comes out in the vitality of her sentences :

"While Hindley and his wife basked downstairs before a comfortable fire—doing anything but reading their Bibles, I'll answer for it—Heathcliff, myself, and the unhappy ploughboy, were commanded to take our Prayer books, and mount : we were ranged in a row, on a sack of corn, groaning and shivering, and hoping that Joseph would shiver too, so that he might give us a short homily for his own sake. A vain idea ! The service lasted precisely three hours; and yet my brother had the face to exclaim, when he saw us descending, 'What, done already?' "

Wit of this sort has a certain maturity : it is poised—"the unhappy ploughboy"—and shrewd—"doing anything but reading their Bibles." Catherine's rebelliousness shows itself here as the humorous reaction of a sympathetic and sensible nature against bullying sentimentality and cant. There is more than the common childish response to love-making in her scorn of Hindley and his Frances.

Passages like this make Catherine quite different from the figure the critics tend to describe. The real Catherine comes across as fully human, sprightly, lovable. She is essentially

normal and even, in the first part of the book, normative. From
the start she is too vital a person to be limited by the conditions
others impose for their own convenience: "her spirits were
always at high-water mark." And she is essentially joyous, with
an expansive sense of life: "singing, laughing, and plaguing
everybody who would not do the same."

The real Heathcliff is evoked by more elusive means; but he
too emerges, at least as a child, as more human than those
around him, more sensitive, more responsive. Lacking Catherine's vivacity, he has nevertheless the most vivid perception
of it:

> "Afterwards, they dried and combed her beautiful hair, and gave her a
> pair of enormous slippers, and wheeled her to the fire; and I left her, as
> merry as she could be, dividing her food between the little dog and
> Skulker, whose nose she pinched as he ate . . . she is so immeasurably
> superior to them—to everybody on earth, is she not, Nelly?"

The tone and rhythm here perfectly render both the speaker
and the actions he describes: his delight wins our consent even
while the last phrases place the feeling as, though true and
touching, a child's.

Nelly remarks several times on the hardness and insensi-
bility of the child Heathcliff. Actually, he feels more deeply
than anyone. His vitality is an inward as Catherine's is an outward fire. Because Nelly is a biased narrator, this can sometimes
be brought out only indirectly, by subtle touches: for example,
the dumb, desolate poignancy of his hurt after Catherine, returning from her stay at the Lintons, first rebuffs him. Nelly
finds him "smoothing the glossy coat of the new pony in the
stable, and feeding the other beasts according to custom." He
remains at the work till nine o'clock at night, then marches
"dumb and dour" to his chamber. Nelly interprets this as ill-
humour. We may see in it a boy's heartbreak and loneliness.

II

A number of critics have thought of Nelly Dean as representing a standard of normality in *Wuthering Heights*, as indicating
the writer's own attitude to the main characters and events, and
as voicing the judgments upon them of conventional morality.
Others have noted that neither of the two main narrators, Lockwood and Nelly, is capable of interpreting the story adequately.
G. D. Klingopulos hints at this dissatisfaction: "Nelly is conventional and . . . her moralizing is rarely quite to the point."
D. A. Traversi is similarly diffident: "Nelly Dean, whose
common sense offers throughout a necessary counterweight, a
relevant though not a final comment."[14] Arnold Kettle makes
the point more perceptively and firmly:

> "The roles of the two narrators . . . are not casual. Their function
> (they the two most 'normal' people in the book) is partly to keep the story
> close to the earth to make it believable, partly to comment on it from a
> common-sense point of view and thereby to reveal in part the inadequacy
> of such common sense."[15]

That is—to develop the point more fully—the novel uses
several narrators (in fact, five or six) to place the story in perspective, or in a variety of perspectives; but it also reverses the
process, and the direction of interest, by making their responses
to the story cast light upon the narrators themselves (even
Zillah's character is richly, though economically, created). To
break down resistance to its central experience, the novel must
somehow overcome the reader's contrary assumptions: it does
so by demonstrating the inadequacy of those assumptions in
Lockwood and Nelly.

Nelly is not merely a witness. She is a creature of will, and
she exerts this will to some effect. Her narrative is deeply
coloured not only by her "conventional values" but also by her

---

[14] *The Pelican Guide to English Literature*, 6 (Dickens to Hardy).
[15] *An Introduction to the English Novel*.

private motives: her personal loyalties and her need to protect herself. This is true of others as well. There is a constant suggestion of bias in the narration, leading at times to incompatible versions of what happened. All the narration involves recollection, selection, and emphasis; and the author shows a keen awareness of how the personality of the speaker may rearrange and even falsify what actually occurred. Catherine's quarrel with Isabella provides a simple but striking example. Isabella declares that she loves Heathcliff "more than ever you loved Edgar." As Catherine repeats the remark to Heathcliff, three pages further on, the insinuation against herself is transposed to Edgar. She becomes not a wife who loves weakly but one who is weakly loved: "Isabella swears that the love Edgar has for me is nothing to that she entertains for you." In case the reader should fail to see the discrepancy, the next sentence reads: "I'm sure she made some speech of the kind; did she not, Ellen?"

Nelly is not an objective observer. She is an active participant in the events she describes—how often a decisive turn is given to the story through her interference or her negligence—and her feelings are deeply engaged. At the very start of her tale she reveals her indentification with the family she used to serve: "Miss Cathy is of us—I mean of the Lintons." Her bias against Heathcliff is manifest equally early. She admits that her conduct towards him when he first arrived was cowardly and inhuman, that she and Hindley hated him and plagued him shamefully. But she never properly faces the implications of these admissions or draws the right conclusions from them. Instead, she sums up Heathcliff's introduction to the family by saying: "So, from the very beginning, he bred bad feeling in the house." This, after describing his patience under Hindley's blows and her pinches.

Nelly's "slanting" is pretty obvious at the start, and not difficult for the alert reader to cope with. Later, it demands greater attentiveness, more of looking backwards and forwards to verify what she says, than the narrative *pace* will allow. For example, at the end of Chapter XVII, Nelly says:

> "Hareton, who should now be the first gentleman in the neighbour-hood, was reduced to a state of complete dependence on his father's inveterate enemy; and lives in his own house as a servant, deprived of the advantage of wages, and quite unable to right himself, because of his friendlessness, and his ignorance that he has been wronged."

But how has Hareton been wronged, and by whom? Nelly effectively suggests that Heathcliff has somehow cheated the boy out of his inheritance. Arnold Kettle, for one, is sufficiently impressed to write: "Heathcliff . . . buys out Hindley and reduces him to drunken impotency. . . . He systematically degrades Hareton Earnshaw to servility and illiteracy." The fact, however, is that Hareton's father was far gone in dissipation long before Heathcliff's return; and it was Hindley who insisted that their gambling should continue to the end:

> "Should he offer to leave me, he's a dead man. . . . Am I to lose *all*, without a chance of retrieval? . . . I *will* have it back; and I'll have *his* gold too; and then his blood."

Heathcliff may have encouraged Hindley's mania, but it remains that Hareton was disinherited mainly by his own father's greed and vindictiveness. But these cross-references are four chapters apart, and in a normal reading one is less likely to see that Nelly's imputations are false than merely to feel uneasy about them.

Where two versions of the same event are given, the problem is to determine not *what* happened but, as it were, *how much* happened. For example, as Isabella relates it, when Hindley attempted to kill Heathcliff and failed, Heathcliff "kicked and trampled on him, and dashed his head repeatedly against the flags." On the writing in this scene, Klingopulos comments:

F

The excess of vividness must be taken either as a symptom of immaturity, of insufficiently understood intensity; or as an error of judgment
on the author's part, a failure to recognise that the physical violence and
ruthlessness of Heathcliff had already been established. . . .

Before accepting this judgment, we need to recall that the
excess of vividness, the immaturity or error of judgment, are
not directly the author's. They belong first of all to Isabella.
Later in the novel the episode is referred to again, more temperately. As Heathcliff relates it: "I remember stopping to kick
the breath out of him, and then hurrying upstairs." Thus we
can't be sure what we have seen: an act of gratuitous brutality
by Heathcliff, or an exaggerated impression of it in the immature and prejudiced witness, Isabella.

This kind of analysis, pushed too far, could make the novel
impossibly ambiguous. Effects like those I've pointed to are
plentiful, but they do not obliterate the story. Rather, they make
the reader vaguely mistrustful, cautious in passing judgment.
And they do this especially with reference to the nastier parts
of Heathcliff's conduct, making for uncertainty not only about
how far his behaviour can be justified but also about precisely
what his behaviour is. Judgment of him is inhibited, to a degree,
by the thought that the case against him has been exaggerated
by the bias of the narrators. Some sense of this appears to lie
behind Kettle's comment on the narrators:

They act as a kind of sieve to the story, sometimes a double sieve, which
has the purpose not only of separating off the chaff, but of making us
aware of the difficulty of passing easy judgments. One is left always with
the sense that the last word has not been said.

But this effect—if, as Kettle seems content to do, we carry
the analysis no further—is surely disturbing. It seems too much
like a superior confidence-trick, and we may wonder whether
it helps to account for the nebulousness with which critics
generally refer to this side of the novel.

III

Everyone agrees that the most important thing in *Wuthering Heights*, its central experience, is the love between Catherine and Heathcliff. What to make of it is another matter. Critics often emphasize its strangeness and, in one way or another, contrive to suggest that it is not "love" at all. Some see it as inhuman, demonic, mystical or mythical; some see it as adolescent fantasy, filled with the violence and weakness of immature passion but with the concomitant unreality. Either way, and whether in praise or in blame, the emphasis is put upon the passion's intensity: intensity for its own sake. So, according to G. D. Klingopulos, we must see the value of the novel "in the vitality of the feelings." And the consequence of this, whether intended or not, is a devaluation, an evacuation of significance. "If Emily Brontë has been careful about anything," writes Klingopulos, "she has been most careful not to qualify whatever the Catherine and Heathcliff themes may be taken to mean. For Catherine and Heathcliff are what she set out to say."

It is a perplexing formula: "whatever the themes may be taken to mean." Does this suggest that the novel must be condemned as obscure and ambiguous in its central themes? Or is it the critic's confession of failure to master his subject? Either way, we can't leave it there. For the relationship of Heathcliff and Catherine is not without meaning. The book's continuing appeal lies, I believe, precisely in the sense it gives of paying an unusually full yet legitimate recognition to a natural and normal human emotion. Catherine's most famous declaration of her feelings is an endeavour not so much to convey the strength as to define the nature of her love, and so to win a recognition from Nelly (and, in a sense, from the reader) of its value:

"If all else perished, and *he* remained, I should still continue to be; and if all else remained, and he were annihilated, the universe would turn to a mighty stranger: I should not seem a part of it. My love for Linton is like the foliage in the woods: time will change it, I'm well aware, as winter changes the trees. My love for Heathcliff resembles the eternal rocks beneath: a source of little visible delight, but necessary."

She distinguishes her love for Heathcliff from her love for Linton not as more highly charged but as having a different basis. Her love for Linton grows out of the changeable surface of personality, rather like what D. H. Lawrence, in his essay on Galsworthy, called "the social being . . . swayed . . . by the money-sway, and by the social moral." She loves Linton because he is handsome, and pleasant, and young, and cheerful, and rich, and loves her. Her love for Heathcliff grows out of what, in the same essay, Lawrence called true humanity, the stable core of self we can know only when at one with "the living continuum of the universe." She loves him because she must: it is the deepest impulse of her nature, it is "necessary." Through her feeling for Heathcliff, Catherine discovers her own identity, her place in the world—as he does through her. The essential quality of their relationship is not its intensity but its perfect, its final, sincerity.

Beside the love of Catherine and Heathcliff all other relationships in the novel pale into insignificance, not only because it is intense and enduring but precisely because it *is* significant, it recognizes important realities of our existence. A world kept in focus only by ignoring those realities would be desperately impoverished.

Lockwood's presence in the novel is best understood, I think, as enforcing just this perception. When he has heard the first part of the story, he reflects on the contrast between these people and people like himself:

They *do* live more in earnest, more in themselves, and less in surface change, and frivolous external things. I could fancy a love for life here almost possible.

That "almost" conveys the whole case. Lockwood is a purely social being, all but incapable of imagining and terrified of encountering the realities of emotional life. The anecdote about his love-affair at the sea-side plainly reveals this. He says that the reputation it earned for him of "deliberate heartlessness" is undeserved. In fact, however, only the one word "deliberate" is undeserved. He is incapable of spontaneous emotion. His feelings are factitious, fashionable, literary: "I was thrown into the company of a most fascinating creature: a real goddess in my eyes, as long as she took no notice of me. I 'never told my love' vocally. . . ." He is afraid of love. He can approach it only when it is kept at a safe distance. When it is offered, he beats a hasty retreat.

This deliberate contrast between the emotional frigidity represented by Lockwood and the vitality of the novel's central experience suggests an attempt to do more than simply present the intense emotion. The novel does not (its form ensures that it cannot) argue or exhort or philosophize. But into its conception there has gone a distillation of thought whose operation can be felt everywhere in the shaping of the material. Wordsworthian in quite a number of ways, *Wuthering Heights* is not the least so in its capacity of assimilating ideas into the presented experience.

IV

> Blest the Babe,
> Nursed in his Mother's arms, who sinks to sleep
> Rocked on his Mother's breast; who with his soul
> Drinks in the feelings of his Mother's eye!
> For him, in one dear Presence, there exists
> A virtue which irradiates and exalts
> Objects through widest intercourse of sense.
> No outcast he, bewildered and depressed:
> Along his infant veins are interfused

The gravitation and the filial bond
Of nature that connect him with the world.

(*The Prelude*)

Heathcliff's love for Catherine is inextricably involved in the
motives of his long-drawn-out struggle for mastery over his
enemies. The two concerns are kept alive together until just
before the end, and the survival of the love must be understood—or puzzled over—along with the perpetuation of the
struggle. The meaning of the one provides the motive for the
other.

The love begins in childhood and rebellion, and its genesis
explains its nature. Heathcliff, the outcast, rejected and humili-
ated, is accepted only by Catherine—herself an orphan; but by
her he is accepted entirely. They recognize in each other their
true humanity, their worth and dignity as persons, their right
to be. Only through this relationship can either of them feel the
vital bond with existence, the sense of belonging, the human
necessity for which is expressed in Catherine's "surely you and
everybody have a notion that there is or should be an existence
of yours beyond you." The loss of exactly this sense is at the
heart of the agony in such modern novels as *Lord Jim* and
Women in Love. And this is the loss that Catherine, through
her wrong choice in marriage, must undergo:

> "Supposing at twelve years old I had been wrenched from the Heights
> and every early association, and my all in all, as Heathcliff was at that
> time, and been converted at a stroke into Mrs. Linton, the lady of Thrush-
> cross Grange, and the wife of a stranger: an exile, and outcast, thence-
> forth from what had been my world—you may fancy a glimpse of the
> abyss where I grovelled!"

Catherine's tragedy is that from deeply fulfilling relationship, from the sense of *community*, she is seduced by the attractive glitter of mere *society*. The point is given its full profundity
in Heathcliff's image of Edgar's inadequacy:

"He might as well plant an oak in a flowerpot, and expect it to thrive, as imagine he can restore her to vigour in the soil of his shallow cares!"

The suggestion here is of more than Catherine's superior vitality: it points towards the need for deep roots into the processes of living, for relationship not with elements artificially isolated and contained but, as it were, with the whole earth.

The singleness of Heathcliff's bond with the world is a central fact of the story. It is as well, therefore, to note that this is a condition imposed on him by the nature of the people he falls among, rather than a product simply of his own perverse will. He does have, at least for some time, a natural eagerness for a wider community of affection. As late as his homecoming after Catherine's marriage, he is disappointed by Nelly's lack of welcome and reproaches her for it: "Nelly, you are not glad!" But Nelly is for the most part hardened against him, and he grows hard in turn. Even so, he turns to her more than once, later in the novel, as something human to share the burden of his experience.

Catherine's apparent withdrawal of this fundamental recognition, her rejection of himself in his degraded circumstances, drives Heathcliff to run away. Her restoration of it, on his return, moves him to go on living instead of taking revenge on Hindley, as he had planned, and then doing away with himself. He seeks revenge on Hindley, and later on Edgar, precisely because they have tried to deny him this recognition. Edgar attempts to deprive Heathcliff of Catherine. That is by far the most important point, but it is not the only one. Edgar as a child had held Heathcliff in such unthinking contempt as to refer to him, without malice, as though he were an object unfit to be directly spoken to, not a person with feelings. When they are grown up Edgar continues to see Heathcliff, despite the improvements in his appearance and bearing, as an inferior and interloper: a "low ruffian." It is difficult to see on what other grounds he can claim knowledge of Heathcliff's "miserable, degraded character," or why he should on such extreme terms forbid Isabella to encourage Heathcliff's advances.

This close relationship of the love and revenge motives gives unity to Heathcliff's story—a complex unity summed up for Heathcliff in all that Hareton seems to personify:

> "Hareton's aspect was the ghost of my immortal love; of my wild endeavours to hold my right; my degradation, my pride, my happiness, and my anguish."

The best discussion of this part of the novel, to my mind, is in Arnold Kettle's *Introduction to the English Novel*. This is one of the rare attempts to treat of Heathcliff's revenge in human terms, and with a proper consciousness of the obligation to make unequivocal judgments; nevertheless it does not seem sufficiently clear and convincing. Like so many others, Kettle gives an overcharged and inaccurate account of Heathcliff's doings:

> Heathcliff becomes a monster: what he does to Isabella, to Hareton, to Cathy, to his son, even to the wretched Hindley, is cruel and inhuman beyond normal thought. He seems concerned to achieve new refinements of horror, new depths of degradation.

Despite these exaggerations, Kettle observes that we "continue to sympathize with Heathcliff . . . to identify ourselves with him *against* the other characters." His explanation is that Heathcliff's revenge has a moral force:

> For what Heathcliff does is to use against his enemies with complete ruthlessness their own weapons, to turn on them . . . their own standards, to beat them at their own game . . . we recognize a rough moral justice in what he has done to his oppressors.

Rough justice: an eye for an eye, tit for tat. Clearly, this won't do. Two wrongs don't make a right. The simple retort of ordinary morality is crushing. We need something better to explain the persistence of sympathy with Heathcliff.

Considering how much emphasis they lay on Heathcliff's ferocity, it seems odd that so little is said by critics about Hindley's. Hindley's brutality, tyranny, and murderous violence far outdo anything of which Heathcliff can be accused on the evidence. Heathcliff, of course, is at the centre of interest, and Hindley is not; but there is another, an interior, difference in the way we see them. Hindley is morally uninteresting; Heathcliff's violence and cruelty by contrast are not random and irresponsible, they are willed. Heathcliff acts with system and forethought. He has certain goals—power, money, a triumph over the circumstances and agents of his former humiliation—and he uses force and deceit to reach them. Where Hindley's violence is wild and unmeasured, Heathcliff's is controlled by purpose. He is only as harsh as the carrying out of his schemes makes necessary. Hindley used to beat Heathcliff. Heathcliff does not beat or bully Hareton. Hanging up Isabella's dog in such a way that it could neither make a noise nor follow them was an essential precaution before their elopement. His other deeds, except under extreme provocation, are likewise controlled.

Heathcliff's conduct, then, must be judged in the light of his purpose. If we do continue to sympathize with him, I suggest that it is because we see, however dimly, what his purpose is, and accept it as giving a moral theme to his actions. We do know what he means by his wild endeavours to hold his *right*. His struggle against his enemies is justified—as far as it is— by the superior right for which he strives. He strives to assert what they so cruelly, and casually, have denied : his right to exist, to hold a place in the scheme of things. So complete and complacent has been their assumption that he belongs to an inferior order of being that only the complete upheaval of their world can redress the balance. Our sympathy is drawn by the struggle of life to triumph over killing contempt.

Dr. Kettle may be right to see a reflection of the Victorian class-struggle in this part of the novel, but to emphasize it would be a mistake. Heathcliff's differences from, say, the Linton family are more than social. A fundamental distinction is suggested between different kinds of being, different kinds of men. "Whatever our souls are made of," says Catherine, "his and mine are the same; and Linton's is as different as a moonbeam from lightning, or frost from fire." The society of the novel is created in the image of the Lintons, its values and its laws are theirs (not for nothing are we told that Edgar is a magistrate), and it does not willingly tolerate the otherness of a Heathcliff. But it is in the recognition and affirmation of diversity, rather than in any emotional plangency, that the novel comes closest to what is valuable in the Romantic tradition to which it belongs. It might have taken for motto Blake's proverb: "One law for the lion and ox is oppression."

For all this, in Heathcliff's behaviour there is an excess from which moral sympathy does turn away: the kind of thing exemplified in: "The more the worms writhe, the more I yearn to crush out their entrails." As a more subtle and convincing instance we may take the savage feeling to which he admits, apropos of the younger Catherine, for anything that seems afraid of him. To regard the revenge-story as simply a moral action would be wrong, for in it the psychological effect of the enjoyment of power provides another theme. It is easy to see how Heathcliff comes by these feelings. To evaluate them, to see how they affect the implied moral judgments in the novel, is not so easy. What they show is that the author never reduces her vision to a diagram, a two-dimensional moral fable. She remains aware that the moral equations are less complex than the human agents. But that the moral judgments are not radically upset may be demonstrated by a contrast. D. A. Traversi points out that the Lintons are capable of "a cruelty which, although very different from Heathcliff's brutality, is hardly less inhuman." Yes; and more. Isabella, at least, has a desire for revenge that matches Heathcliff's own. Hers is truly a thirst for rough justice: "an eye for an eye, a tooth for a tooth; for every wrench of agony return a wrench." But this, as Isabella's spiteful impotence betrays, possesses no moral force: it is too negative. Heathcliff strives to triumph over his enemies, she only to "reduce him to my level." In that betraying phrase we see perhaps the subtlest variation on the novel's theme.

Nelly Dean and
the Power of
"Wuthering Heights"*

JOHN K. MATHISON

THE MEMORABLE quality of *Wuthering Heights*, its power, has often been mentioned; numerous elements of the work have been considered the source of this power. No one element can be expected to account completely for it, and no combination of causes is likely to produce an answer that is fully satisfying. But examinations of the various elements in the structure of the novel have suggested clear connections between method and results, between technique and meaning.[1]

* © 1956 by The Regents of the University of California. Reprinted from *Nineteenth-Century Fiction*, volume XI, pp. 106–129, by permission of The Regents.

[1] I shall make no attempt to refer to previous studies of *Wuthering Heights* in the course of my essay. The essays listed below, as well as others, have all given readers valuable help in elucidating various causes of the power of the novel. My own essay does not intend to challenge or refute any of them, but to make one further suggestion towards this elucidation, through the consideration of one other aspect in detail. For criticism of *Wuthering Heights* from the time of its publication until 1948, one may consult Melvin R. Watson, "*Wuthering Heights* and the Critics," *The Trollopian*, III (1948), 243–263. Another article by Mr. Watson, "Tempest in the Soul: The Theme and Structure of *Wuthering Heights*," NCF, IV (1949), 87–100, in comparing the structure of the novel to that of an Elizabethan play, and in considering Nelly Dean technically valuable as a means of dividing the action into convenient acts, has a closer bearing on my essay. Other essays which give some consideration to Nelly Dean are: William E. Buckler, "Chapter VII of *Wuthering Heights*: A Key to Interpretation," NCF, VII (1952), 51–55; Boris Ford, "*Wuthering Heights*," *Scrutiny*, VII (1939), 375–

In this essay I am attempting a partial explanation of the power of the book through a detailed examination not of the general question of the use of a narrator but specifically of the fully developed character of Nelly Dean. Nelly Dean is not a mere technical device: we cannot forget as the story progresses that we are hearing it from her rather than from the author. She is a minute interpreter. She tells us what events mean, what is right or wrong, what is praiseworthy or despicable or unforgivable behaviour. Her morality is a result of her training, experiences, and reading, combined with her native temperament. The reader's degree of acceptance of her explanations and moral judgments determines his understanding of the meaning of the story and its power over him.

Nelly is an admirable woman whose point of view, I believe, the reader must reject. She is good-natured, warmhearted, wholesome, practical, and physically healthy. Her interpretation of her reading and her experiences, her feelings on various occasions, are, to a large extent, the consequence of her physical health. When the reader refuses to accept her view of things, which he continually does and must do, he is forced to feel the

389; and Dorothy Van Ghent, "On *Wuthering Heights*," *The English Novel, Form and Function* (New York: Rinehart, 1953), pp. 153–170. Two other essays particularly valuable in the elucidation of *Wuthering Heights* are G. D. Klingopulos, "The Novel as Dramatic Poem (II): 'Wuthering Heights,'" *Scrutiny*, XIV (1947), 269–286, and Mark Schorer, "Fiction and the Matrix of Analogy," *Kenyon Review*, XI (1949), 539–560. Mr. Klingopulos asserts that "the author's preferences are not shown, do not reveal themselves unambiguously even to analysis" (p. 271). Mr. Schorer, in a very convincing demonstration of the consequences of the metaphorical language in a work of fiction, believes that Emily Brontë reached a conclusion she did not quite intend. "At the end the voice that drones on is the perdurable voice of the country, Nelly Dean's. No more than Heathcliff did Emily Brontë quite intend that homespun finality" (p. 549). It is not necessary to explain the ways in which my analysis differs from these in this note. Finally, three other essays should be mentioned: Richard Chase, "The Brontës, or Myth Domesticated," *Forms of Modern Fiction*, ed. William Van O'Connor (Minneapolis: University of Minnesota Press, 1948), pp. 102–119; C. P. Sanger, "The Structure of *Wuthering Heights*," *The Hogarth Essays*, XIX (London: Hogarth Press, 1926), 24 pp.; and Dorothy Van Ghent, "The Window Figure and the Two-Children Figure in *Wuthering Heights*," *NCF*, VII (1952), 189–197.

inadequacy of the normal, healthy, hearty, good-natured person's understanding of life and human nature. He is consequently forced into an active participation in the book. He cannot sit back and accept what is given him as the explanation of the actions of the characters. He must continually provide his own version.

For the reader to disagree with Nelly would be easy, if Nelly were not admirable. But to prevent the reader's turning Nelly into a cliché of simple and narrow piety, Emily Brontë has provided Joseph. He makes clear through his actions and his explicit statements to Nelly that she is not conventionally or rigidly pious. Her condemnations and approvals do not result from an unintelligent or fanatical acceptance of rigid rules of conduct. Joseph is sure she is destined for hell because of her warmth and human kindness, and because of her enjoyment of such pleasures as folk song and dancing. Joseph's strictures intensify the reader's favourable impressions of Nelly, the favourable impressions that make his rejection of her views more intense and significant.

And enough other servants are introduced to increase still further our realization of Nelly's superiority, intellectual and moral. Her pipe-smoking successor at the Grange[2] is apparently what might be expected of a servant. One need not more than mention Zillah, who has some mental alertness, to be made strongly aware of Nelly's superiority.

But more strongly than her superiority is shown by contrast with Joseph, with Zillah, or with the servant Lockwood finds at the Grange on his return, it is shown by the affection of the major characters, including Heathcliff, for her, as seen not in their words but in their behaviour to her. And of course there is her narrative, full as it is of her ideas. In spite of all her fine

---

[2] *Wuthering Heights*, p. 324. This page reference and all subsequent ones are to the Rinehart Edition with an Introduction by Mark Schorer.

qualities, nevertheless, she fails to understand the other characters and, more important, fails in her behaviour in important crises of the action. From the emphasis on her admirable qualities, and from her final inadequacy, the reader is led to see that the insight of the normal, wholesome person cannot penetrate into all feelings justly: the reader becomes the active advocate of the extremes of passion of Cathy and Heathcliff, troublesome as they are to a peaceful, domestic routine.

Emily Brontë could not have succeeded in a direct attempt to demand our sympathy for or understanding of two such characters as Heathcliff and Cathy. Approached directly, the reader would not have to exercise his own perceptions; he would remain passive. Some readers might say that such violent behaviour is exciting enough to read about in romantic novels, but that in real life it would not do to encourage such people as Cathy and Heathcliff. To other readers, the novel might have appeared merely as a tremendous protest against conventional standards, but the interest in it would be merely biographical, sociological, or psychological.

By indirection, Emily Brontë has produced not a personal protest but a work of art. The reader's reaction is not, of course, the precise opposite of any of those mentioned above, not a simple stamp of approval bestowed on Heathcliff and Cathy, but a realization that the "normal" person is often incapable of feeling for the tortured, emotionally distraught person, and that the latter's tortured failure to understand himself and the sources of his misery partly results from the failure of imagination of the majority. The question is not whether Heathcliff and Cathy are good or bad. They are the result of psychological isolation and misunderstanding working on a particular native temperament, and the "good" are as much the doers of the damage as the "bad," either Hindley or Joseph.

The better we come to know Nelly, the more we recognize

her lack of understanding of the principals. To know her we need to watch her character as it is revealed through her opinions, and even more, through her reports of her own actions. It is this person, whom we come to know well, whose judgments we finally interpret. Not abstract judgments of a merely nominal narrator, they are the particular limited judgments of a person of a distinct emotional and intellectual viewpoint. Knowing the judge, or interpreter, knowing the giver of advice as well as the advice given, we realize the inadequacy of the interpretation, the advice, and the judgments; we become as we read active interpreters, protesters, explicators, and possibly judges.

II

Nelly's physical vigour is emphatically part of her character. Impressing us generally from her account of her actions throughout the novel, her abundant good health is specifically alluded to as well. Her one illness, a bad cold after she had been obliged to sit for a long while in "soaked shoes and stockings," was a great surprise to her; up to the time of the narrative it is the only indisposition in her life that she can recall. By this accident, which most would accept as in the course of things, her spirits were depressed: "It is wearisome, to a stirring active body—but few have slighter reasons for complaint than I had" (p. 257). Elsewhere, responding to the terrors of Cathy, who fears that everyone she knows may die and leave her alone, Nelly confidently boasts: ". . . I am strong, and hardly forty-five. My mother lived till eighty, a canty dame to the last" (p. 244). Numerous examples of illness, decline, wasting away, and death in her experience make little impression on her, who feels herself so strong. Although she once remarks "I am stout, and soon put out of breath" (p. 286), this reference confirms rather than contradicts her feeling of "ruddy" health; the picture is that of the Shepherd's wife in *The Winter's Tale*:

> when my old wife liv'd, upon
> This day she was both pantler, butler, cook;
> Both dame and servant; welcom'd all, serv'd all,
> Would sing her song and dance her turn; now here,
> At upper end o' the table, now i' the middle;
> On his shoulder, and his; her face o' fire
> With labour and the thing she took to quench it . . .
>   (IV, iii, 55–61)

Her own health makes her a poor sympathizer with the illnesses of others; she tends to view even those illnesses in the novel which end in death as partly wilful, partly acting. The physique and the temperament which goes with it of the weak or sick she cannot really believe in. An early example is her view of Hindley's consumptive wife; throughout the book further examples abound, to the last case of the frail son of Isabella whom she finds revolting largely because he will not exert himself and be vigorous. But to resume, of Hindley's wife, who had expressed fear of dying, she says:

> I imagined her as little likely to die as myself. She was rather thin, but young, and fresh complexioned, and her eyes sparkled as bright as diamonds. I did remark, to be sure, that mounting the stairs made her breathe very quick, that the least sudden noise set her all in a quiver, and that she coughed troublesomely sometimes: but, I knew nothing of what these symptoms portended, and had no impulse to sympathize with her. We don't in general take to foreigners here, Mr. Lockwood, unless they take to us first (pp. 46–47).

Since Nelly regards the idea of her own death as absurd, she sees no reason that Hindley's wife should be entitled to a fear of death. Such nonsense is just what one expects of foreigners (from a different county of England). This passage, very early in the novel, makes the reader aware of Nelly's fallibility of

G

judgment combined with her satisfaction with her own attitudes. It conditions our expectations regarding her probable actions in later episodes, and helps us know her and hence discount her judgments and substitute our own. These early suspicions are confirmed when Cathy becomes ill:

> . . . Mr. Kenneth, as soon as he saw her, pronounced her dangerously ill; she had a fever.
> He bled her, and he told her to let her live on whey, and water gruel; and take care she did not throw herself down stairs, or out of the window; and then he left. . . .
> Though I cannot say I made a gentle nurse, and Joseph and the master were no better; and though our patient was as wearisome and headstrong as a patient could be, she weathered it through (p. 92).

Why should Cathy have chosen to come down with a fever, become dangerously delirious, and consequently be "wearisome" to healthy, reasonable people?

If we knew less of Nelly we might be able to sympathize with her jogging of Lockwood during his illness: " 'You shouldn't lie till ten. There's the very prime of the morning gone long before that time. A person who has not done one half his day's work by ten o'clock, runs a chance of leaving the other half undone' " (p. 64). As it is, however, we know her advice is little more than justification of her own natural urges to be "busy and stirring" always; it is her failure to grasp the possibility of people's being less vigorous than herself.

Most serious is her deficiency in Cathy's later illness and delirium, foreshadowed by the illness already mentioned. Inevitably, she views it as an act:

> "Catherine ill?" he [Edgar Linton] said, hastening to us. "Shut the window, Ellen! Catherine! why . . ."
> He was silent; the haggardness of Mrs. Linton's appearance smote him speechless, and he could only glance from her to me in horrified astonishment.
> "She's been fretting here," I continued, "and eating scarcely anything,

and never complaining, she would admit none of us till this evening, and so we couldn't inform you of her state, as we were not aware of it ourselves, *but it is nothing*" [italics mine] (pp. 134–135).

One might suppose Ellen's "it is nothing" were a well-meant if unsuccessful effort to cheer Edgar, if the scene ended at this point, and if we had not begun to know Nelly rather well, but as it continues, it becomes clear that she really considers the illness both wilful and minor:

"Her mind wanders, sir," I interposed. "She has been talking nonsense the whole evening; but let her have quiet and proper attendance, and she'll rally. Hereafter, we must be cautious how we vex her."
"I desire no further advice from you," answered Mr. Linton. "You knew your mistress's nature, and you encouraged me to harass her. And not to give me one hint of how she has been these three days! It was heartless! Months of sickness could not cause such a change!"
I began to defend myself, thinking it too bad to be blamed for another's wicked waywardness! (pp. 135–136).

As Edgar Linton says, Nelly had had a lifetime of experience with Cathy, but the last quoted sentence alone makes clear the triumph of constitution and temperament over experience. Nelly never will grasp the less wholesome, physically or emotionally.

It may need to be said that objectively it would be possible for the reader to find Cathy a difficult person. But the healthy Nelly's complacent self-justification and lack of surmise of stronger passions and more highly strung temperaments, make the reader Cathy's advocate in the context, and while he reads they lower his enthusiasm for the vigorously normal and, it appears, consequently obtuse.

Nelly's health is only one, though a significant, feature of the total character. Her "philosophy" on all sorts of matters is presented in detail. It is primarily a matter of avoiding any really strong passions, but continually encouraging a good deal of "natural affection." Children must "take to her." On a visit to the Heights she encounters the five-year-old Hareton near the building, and he begins to throw stones at her, and curses, distorting "his baby features into a shocking expression of malignity" (p. 115). Her reaction is unperceptively conventional.

> You may be certain this grieved, more than angered me. Fit to cry, I took an orange from my pocket, and offered it to propitiate him.
> He hesitated, and then snatched it from my hold, as if he fancied I only intended to tempt and disappoint him (p. 115).

Here, too, she is clearly more concerned with her picture of herself as affectionately motherly, than with understanding.

She believes in forgiving one's enemies, but she herself, not having to struggle hard in this respect, does not realize that for others placid domestic normality may not be the strongest drive. After a serious crisis in which Hindley had confined Heathcliff (during childhood) fasting in the garret for more than twenty-four hours, she broke Hindley's commands by letting him into the kitchen to feed him : "he was sick and could eat little . . ."; he remained "wrapt in dumb meditation."

> On my inquiring the subject of his thoughts, he answered gravely—
> "I'm trying to settle how I shall pay Hindley back. I don't care how long I wait, if I can only do it, at last. I hope he will not die before I do !"
> "For shame, Heathcliff !" said I. "It is for God to punish wicked people; we should learn to forgive."
> "No, God won't have the satisfaction that I shall," he returned. "I only wish I knew the best way ! Let me alone, and I'll plan it out : while I'm thinking of that, I don't feel pain."
> But, Mr. Lockwood, I forget these tales cannot divert you. I'm annoyed how I should dream of chattering on at such a rate . . . I could have told Heathcliff's history, all that you need hear, in half a dozen words (p. 63).

Nelly is sorry for Heathcliff and sneaks him some supper. As usual she compromises, helping Heathcliff a little and disobeying Hindley a little. Perhaps that is what was possible. But in her role as narrator she looks back upon the event, having seen the whole history of the subsequent years, and takes it in stride, still blaming Heathcliff conventionally for his lapses, still blaming others moderately, and still keeping her picture of herself as normally affectionate and good. Heathcliff should have listened to her and forgiven his enemies.

She allows, of course, for normal selfishness. Since the marriage of Cathy to Edgar Linton does take place, she hopefully finds signs that there is a "deep and growing happiness" in their union. At least she is able to be a bustling housekeeper; there are no domestic storms. But this happy period ended. "Well, we *must* be for ourselves in the long run; the mild and generous are only more justly selfish than the domineering—and it ended when circumstances caused each to feel that the one's interest was not the chief consideration in the other's thoughts" (p. 97). To her this situation is normal. No allowance is made for the enduring passion of Cathy and Heathcliff. No doubt Cathy's marriage would have appeared more successful had she forgotten Heathcliff, but it is too easy for Nelly to take this stand for the reader to go along with her. He begins to sympathize with the course that Cathy and Heathcliff did take.

Later when the reader might have been exasperated with a tantrum of Cathy's, Nelly's stolidity makes him take Cathy's part against the printed interpretation:

The stolidity with which I received these instructions was, no doubt, rather exasperating; for they were delivered in perfect sincerity; but I believed a person who could plan the turning of her fits of passion to account, beforehand, might, by exerting her will, manage to control herself tolerably even while under their influence; and I did not wish to "frighten" her husband, as she said, and multiply his annoyances for the purpose of serving her selfishness (p. 124).

For Nelly to control "fits of passion" and "manage to control herself while under their influence" have never required a struggle. She is too ruddy, healthy, physically busy and emotionally placid to know what such a struggle would be. When a few pages later she confidently announces that "the Grange had but one sensible soul in its walls, and that lodged in my body" (p. 127), we agree, but the value we place on being "sensible" is far lower than hers.

Nelly is as much opposed to cold lack of visible affection as to violent passion. Normally approving of Edgar Linton, she fails to understand the feeling behind his apparent coldness and is quite ready to condemn him in his treatment of Isabella:

> "And you won't write her a little note, sir?" I asked imploringly.
> "No," he answered. "It is needless. My communication with Heathcliff's family shall be as sparing as his with mine. It shall not exist!"
> Mr. Edgar's coldness depressed me exceedingly; and all the way from the Grange, I puzzled my brains how to put more heart into what he said, when I repeated it; and how to soften his refusal of even a few lines to console Isabella (p. 155).

She is "depressed" by "coldness," although all she wants from Edgar is a few futilely affectionate, meaningless, brotherly words not calculated to achieve any helpful result. That there is more "heart" in his coldness than in her superficiality does not occur to her. To make things well, and it really seems so to those like her, she will soften his refusal, in some compromising way, and thus receive the congratulations of her own conscience. On arriving at the Heights a few minutes later, she is actually able to say, "There never was such a dreary, dismal scene as the *formerly cheerful* house presented" [italics mine] (pp. 155–156).

The reader's first view of the house had been Lockwood's on his first visit, the history Nelly has told started with the discord resulting from the introduction into the house of the orphan Heathcliff (and the reactions to this say little enough in favour of the Earnshaws), and he has subsequently been concerned with Heathcliff, Cathy, and their agonized growing up in the

house, not to mention Hindley, Joseph, and Hindley's consumptive wife. The reader, consequently, cannot help placing a low
value on the judgment of the wholesome Nelly, and he re-
assesses her narrative with quite a different emphasis.

Edgar, except for his coldness to Isabella, is admired by Nelly.
No unleashed and distressing passions are usually his, but a
sensible and quiet affection, comforting to the housekeeper. Referring to Edgar's mourning for his deceased wife, Nelly approvingly says: "But he was too good to be thoroughly unhappy long. *He* didn't pray for Catherine's soul to haunt him:
Time brought resignation, and a melancholy sweeter than common joy. He recalled her memory with ardent, tender love,
and hopeful aspiring to the better world, where, he doubted
not, she was gone" (p. 194). How much of this is Nelly's attribution and how much was Edgar's real state remain doubtful;
surely the part about "melancholy sweeter than common joy"
is something she picked up from her boasted reading in the
Linton library, but much is her natural wholesomely senti-
mental feeling about the decorous way for a bereaved husband
to act. Possibly, too, Emily Brontë is indicating a tendency in
Nelly to show off her elegance to impress Lockwood, a gentleman.

Of those aspects of experience which threaten to upset her
outlook she forbids discussion, admitting her uneasiness, but
willing to push aside the difficulty. Cathy, wishing to reveal a
seriously troubling dream to Nelly, is abruptly halted: "'Oh!
don't, Miss Catherine!' I cried. 'We're dismal enough without
conjuring up ghosts and visions to perplex us. Come, come, be
merry, and like yourself! Look at little Hareton—*he's* dreaming
nothing dreary. How sweetly he smiles in his sleep!'" (p. 84).
Apart from the unwillingness to hear the dream, for Nelly to
characterize Cathy as "merry, and like yourself" is a stretch in
making the desired the actual at any time during Cathy's

adolescence, and her preference for babies is again apparent. Cathy replies: "'Yes; and how sweetly his father curses in his solitude! You remember him, I dare say, when he was just such another as that chubby thing—nearly as young and innocent'" (p. 84). Nelly interrupted her story to explain the situation to Lockwood:

> I was superstitious about dreams then, and am still; and Catherine had an unusual gloom in her aspect, that made me dread something from which I might shape a prophecy, and foresee a dreadful catastrophe.
> She was vexed, but she did not proceed. Apparently taking up another subject, she recommenced in a short time.
> "If I were in heaven, Nelly, I should be extremely miserable."
> "Because you are not fit to go there," I answered. "All sinners would be miserable in heaven."
> "But it is not for that. I dreamt, once, that I was there."
> "I tell you I won't hearken to your dreams, Miss Catherine! I'll go to bed," I interrupted again (p. 84).

Little help can the distracted girl get from the only one from whom she can even try to get it. Nothing must interfere with Nelly's determination to impose her own meaning on events, and that meaning must be ordinary and cheerful. But Cathy and Heathcliff persist in a fatal tendency to try to confide in Nelly. Even at the end of his life Heathcliff confesses to her, although, dreading to hear anything unsettlingly appalling, she half refuses to listen.

The customary always triumphs with Nelly. Admirable feelings in Heathcliff, if strange or uncustomary, are shut out of her mind. Far from admirable attitudes in Edgar are approved without question, if they would be shared by most normal people in his station. When Isabella is attracted to Heathcliff, Nelly observes it merely as a new trouble to Edgar: "Leaving aside the degradation of an alliance with a nameless man, and the possible fact that his property, in default of heirs male, might pass into such a one's power, he had sense to comprehend

Heathcliff's disposition . . ." (p. 106). No reader can approve such merely conventional objections, introduced without a qualm. Such attitudes had been responsible for much of the maiming of Heathcliff already. And Heathcliff is here blamed, as often, merely for not knowing his place.

Nelly is similarly imperceptive when Isabella, who has really suffered from Heathcliff, reviles him. Nelly's attempt is simply to "hush" her railings. To Isabella's "would that he could be blotted out of creation, and out of my memory!" Nelly replies, "Hush, hush! He's a human being . . . Be more charitable; there are worse men than he is yet!" (p. 183). What appears is her hatred of extremes; she does not want even Heathcliff to be unique, but merely a normally bad man, one of the well-known class of sinners. What she advocates is some conventional verbal charity and to forget, to proceed as if nothing had happened.

Nelly is a woman whom everyone in her circle, employers, the children of employers, the other servants in the neighbour-hood, the people of Gimmerton, and Lockwood have recog-nized as superior, and admirable. How superior to Joseph, Zillah, and to various other characters the reader readily per-ceives. To insist that she should have shown a full understand-ing of Cathy and Heathcliff would be to show a lack of under-standing of what is possible or probable. From day to day she did her best, with regard to her own welfare and peace of com-fort; few would have done better.

None the less, her character, a representation of the normal at its best, is inadequate to the situation. As will be shown, fail-ing to understand them, she advises them poorly, and her actions in relation to them are also harmful. Emily Brontë does not plead for them. She lets us see them as they were seen and dealt with by a good woman. The reader must progressively lower his estimate of the value of the normal and healthy, de-velop a comprehension of and sympathy for genuine emotions however extreme and destructive, and in so doing become an active interpreter of the meaning of the novel. The reader's active involvement and sympathy with the conventionally despicable makes the power of the book.

III

Resulting from qualities in themselves admirable, Nelly's judgments based on her understanding of events and other people result in advice and action which are parts of the total harm done to Cathy and Heathcliff. Describing the first days of Heathcliff in the Earnshaw household, she makes it apparent to the reader that her presence there will do nothing to better the little Heathcliff's situation. Speaking of the child's silent endurance of Hindley's torments, she says:

> This endurance made old Earnshaw furious when he discovered his son persecuting the poor, fatherless child, as he called him. He took to Heathcliff strangely believing all he said (for that matter, he said precious little, and generally the truth), and petting him up far above Cathy, who was too mischievous and wayward for a favourite.
>
> So, from the very beginning, he bred bad feeling in the house . . . (p. 38).

Heathcliff is, at this early point in the story, obviously blameless, yet Nelly sides with the persecutors, concerned with the trouble caused by an unusual, and hence somehow wrong situation. Looking back through the years, she can only suppose that all would have been well had Mr. Earnshaw never had so freakish a notion as to introduce a waif into the neighbourhood, not that the waif become warped through continued mistreatment and helpless suffering. The parenthetical words, whose significance she disregards, reveal the almost inevitable obtuseness of interpretation by a person of her type.

One page further on, another anecdote makes a point opposite from what Nelly intends it to. Heathcliff's colt (a gift from old Earnshaw) becoming lame, the boy tries to exchange it for Hindley's sound one. "'You must exchange horses with me; I don't like mine, and if you won't I shall tell your father of the three thrashings you've given me this week, and show him my arm, which is black to the shoulder'" (p. 39). The result is that Hindley "cuffs his ears," then threatens him with an iron weight, which he finally hurls at him, hitting him in the chest. Nelly prevents Heathcliff from revealing this blow to old Earnshaw, and Hindley suddenly says: "'Take my colt, gipsy, then! . . . And I pray that he may break your neck; take him, and be damned, you beggarly interloper! and wheedle my father out of all he has, only afterwards show him what you are, imp of Satan—and take that, I hope he'll kick out your brains!'" (p. 40). Of the words or blows, which were more damaging to young Heathcliff may be debated, but Nelly's actively taking the part of Hindley certainly contributes to the harm. And beyond that, she teaches Heathcliff to lie about the episode; "I persuaded him easily to let me lay the blame of his bruises on the horse; he minded little what tale was told since he had what he wanted. He complained so seldom, indeed of such stirs as these, that I really thought him not vindictive—I was deceived, completely, as you will hear" (p. 40). From the beginning, Nelly deals with Heathcliff through a policy of expediency, preserving outward tranquillity, preventing "stirs" in the family. Later when events demand even more of her, we recollect her habitual patterns of behaviour, and know she will continue to fail, with increasingly serious results.

After old Earnshaw's death when Hindley becomes "Master," Nelly is not much troubled by the resulting deliberate degradation of Heathcliff. "He bore his degradation pretty well at first, because Cathy taught him what she learnt, and worked or played with him in the fields. They both promised fair to grow up as rude as savages . . ." (p. 47). More surprising is her assumption that the fanatical Joseph's discipline would have been successful unless there was something basically wrong with Heathcliff and Cathy: "The curate might set as many chapters as he pleased for Catherine to get by heart, and Joseph might thrash Heathcliff till his arm ached; they forgot everything the minute they were together again, at least the minute they had contrived some naughty plan of revenge . . ." (pp. 47–48). Another of her methods of helping Heathcliff is seen slightly later in a reproof: "'You are incurable, Heathcliff, and Mr. Hindley will have to proceed to extremities, see if he won't'" (p. 53).

Dramatically, with no recourse to the essay technique of Fielding as he restores the wayward Tom Jones to the favour of the reader, the reader's sympathies are being directed powerfully towards Heathcliff, and Cathy. More powerfully, perhaps, because unless he is making a deliberate analysis of the book he does not feel his sympathies being directed by a device of the author. Fielding's reader, directly exhorted, may argue back; Emily Brontë's reader reacts spontaneously in favour of Heathcliff.

The most Nelly can admit is that Hindley was a bad "example" for Heathcliff. This way of going to ruin—evil companions showing the way to vice—is familiar, and she makes allowance for Heathcliff in this way. It is a qualified allowance, for Heathcliff, she says, seemed "possessed of something diabolical at that period" (p. 68). Her evidence is that Heathcliff rejoiced to see Hindley degrade himself. But the portrait of Heathcliff is far from the depravity suggested in miscellaneous remarks:

In the first place, he had, by that time, lost the benefit of his early education: continual hard work, begun soon and concluded late, had extinguished any curiosity he once possessed in pursuit of knowledge, and any love for books or learning. His childhood's sense of superiority, in-

stilled into him by the favours of old Mr. Earnshaw, was faded away.
He struggled long to keep up an equality with Catherine in her studies,
and yielded with poignant though silent regret: but he yielded completely; and there was no prevailing on him to take a step in the way of
moving upward, when he found he must, necessarily, sink beneath his
former level (pp. 70–71).

It is hard to see how Nelly could account for Heathcliff's behaviour at the same time both by diabolical possession and as
she does here, but her ability to describe accurately, and yet disregard the facts in favour of explanation by a conventional
formula, is a major feature of her character and her inadequacy
as a counsellor.

Usually, of course, Cathy and Heathcliff are being simultaneously influenced. When Cathy returns from her stay at Thrushcross Grange, Nelly is deceived by the surface improvement in
her manners (p. 54). But Heathcliff's consequent desire for re-
form and self-improvement gets discouragingly brisk treatment:

"Nelly, make me decent, I'm going to be good."
"High time, Heathcliff," I said; "you have grieved Catherine; she's
sorry she ever came home, I dare say! It looks as if you envied her, because
she is more thought of than you" (p. 58).

Nelly, complacently quoting herself in such passages, still
realizes no shortcomings in herself (her questions to Lockwood
on moral problems from time to time never touch such failings).
Had Heathcliff told his story, excusing all his actions through
harsh portraits of these adults, the effect would be reversed: the
reader would excuse the adults and blame Heathcliff, saying
that they were no worse than most normal conventional people,
and that others have survived better in worse circumstances.

Nelly's major failure (though few could have done better) is
in the decisive episode during which Cathy reveals her intention
of marrying Linton, despite her lack of love for him, and her
intense love for, her identity with, Heathcliff. Nelly dissembles

her knowledge of Heathcliff's presence, but worse, her knowledge of his departure at the worst possible moment: "Having noticed a slight movement, I turned my head, and saw him rise from the bench, and steal out, noiselessly. He had listened till he heard Catherine say it would degrade her to marry him, and then he stayed to hear no farther" (p. 85). And when Catherine wants to be assured that Heathcliff, unlike herself, does not know what deep love is, Nelly answers equivocally, " 'I see no reason that he should not know, as well as you . . . and if *you* are his choice, he'll be the most unfortunate creature that ever was born!' " (*ibid.*), automatically putting Cathy in the wrong, getting herself over a difficult moment. What this moment has done is let Heathcliff overhear and leave, and the plans for marriage to Edgar go forward; Nelly has not let Cathy know that Heathcliff has heard her say that it would degrade her to marry him, but has not heard her say the words describing her real feelings, leading up to "I am Heathcliff." Nelly's view of the scene, in which her own inconvenience is more important than either Heathcliff's or Cathy's sufferings, is summarized by herself at the conclusion of Cathy's tremendous confession: "She paused, and hid her face in the folds of my gown; but I jerked it forcibly away. I was out of patience with her folly!" (p. 86).

The reader, prepared by earlier passages in which Nelly has shown, on lesser occasions, her inevitable adherence to expediency or her own comfort, is not surprised by the major failure here: moral habits are not likely to be overcome in a crisis where there is little time for struggle and deliberation. Heathcliff enters and leaves while Cathy is talking and Nelly cannot but act from habit, on the spur of the moment, but the defects revealed in this scene are her customary ones. Here, perhaps more than anywhere, the reader is sharply aware not only of her failure as an interpreter of the past, but more important, of her failure as a counsellor at the time of the action. Both failures cooperate to affect the reader and produce the power of the scene.

The following page, on which Nelly admits that Heathcliff had heard much, confirms the disaster: Cathy searches for Heathcliff during the storm, and stays up all night in wet clothes while Nelly, at one here with Joseph, is chiefly concerned about the interruption in the household routine, even after Heathcliff is clearly gone and Cathy has come down with a serious illness. This whole passage, too well remembered to need detailed citation, is the turning-point. We see it as Nelly tells it. Our necessity of disagreeing completely with the narrator's version, made very easy owing to the great detail, gives our total sympathy to Cathy and Heathcliff. We give, perhaps, more than they deserve; we become unduly severe towards Nelly, but to make us feel powerfully the inadequacy of the "steady reasonable kind of body," Emily Brontë's technique could not be improved. Neither a direct plea nor a narrator who was a moralizing, narrow-minded, hypocritically pious guardian could have placed us so completely with Heathcliff and Cathy. It needs above all Nelly's admirable qualities including particularly the affection she arouses in both Cathy and Heathcliff, and the awareness that her failure is the result of them. Heathcliff and Cathy would have fared better with worse parental guidance. The failure of the ordinarily good being made apparent, the reader, attempting to supply the fuller comprehension, becomes fully involved in the novel.[3]

---

[3] A very different case of the same fundamental problem is shown with Lady Russell in *Persuasion*. Lady Russell is admirable but has certain qualities (dislike of wit and cleverness, and veneration of position) whch cause her to fail as an adviser to Anne. Unless an admirable character in Anne's original social group had been shown wanting, it would not be clear that Anne was correct in emotionally and intellectually abandoning her family and their values. (Her one regret on marriage is that she has no friends or relations to introduce to Wentworth who will add to his social pleasures.) If she were only abandoning the stand of her absurd father and sister, she could still have accepted the group as Emma did in marrying Knightley. But with the inclusion of Lady Russell, the best type that the group can offer, Anne's revolt from the group itself is complete.

To emphasize the significance of the whole scene, Emily Brontë has Nelly sum up her attitude :

> One day, I had the misfortune, when she provoked me exceedingly, to lay the blame of his disappearance on her (where indeed it belonged, as she well knew). From that period for several months, she ceased to hold any communication with me, save in the relation of a mere servant. Joseph fell under a ban also; he *would* speak his mind, and lecture her all the same as if she were a little girl . . . (p. 93).

Later on, a dialogue between Heathcliff and Nelly emphasizes this superficiality of hers by contrasting her explanation with his. To his inquiry, after Cathy's marriage and illness, concerning her condition, Nelly first replies, "I blamed her, as she deserved, for bringing it all on herself," and continues, "the person [Edgar] who is compelled, of necessity, to be her companion, will only sustain his affection hereafter, by the remembrance of what she once was, by common humanity, and a sense of duty!" She is speaking not out of any true knowledge of Edgar, but out of her determination to edify Heathcliff. His refusal to be edified produces his reply and reveals once more Nelly's inadequacy : " 'That is quite possible,' remarked Heathcliff, forcing himself to seem calm, 'quite possible that your master should have nothing but common humanity and a sense of duty to fall back upon. But do you imagine that I shall leave Catherine to his *duty* and *humanity*? and can you compare my feelings respecting Catherine, to his?' " (p. 157).

Heathcliff finally forces her to agree to arrange an interview between him and Cathy; her motives are not a genuine feeling for the two, but the desire to avoid an "explosion" :

> Was it right or wrong? I fear it was wrong, though expedient. I thought I prevented another explosion by my compliance; and I thought, too, it might create a favourable crisis in Catherine's mental illness : and then I remembered Mr. Edgar's stern rebuke of my carrying tales; and I tried to smooth away all disquietude on the subject, by affirming, with frequent

iteration, that that betrayal of trust, if it merited so harsh an appellation, should be the last (p. 163).

Worse is the smugness in reporting the actual meeting when she sarcastically remarks "it seemed Heathcliff *could* weep on a great occasion like this" (p. 171). And conventionally, she weeps herself for Heathcliff after Cathy's death:

"She's dead!" he said; "I've not waited for you to learn that. Put your handkerchief away—don't snivel before me. Damn you all! she wants none of *your* tears!"

I was weeping as much for him as her: we do sometimes pity creatures that have none of the feeling either for themselves or others; and when I first looked into his face, I perceived that he had got intelligence of the catastrophe; and a foolish notion struck me that his heart was quelled, and he prayed, because his lips moved, and his gaze was bent on the ground.

"Yes, she's dead!" I answered, checking my sobs, and drying my cheeks. "Gone to heaven, I hope, where we may, every one, join her, if we take due warning, and leave our evil ways to follow good!"

"Did *she* take due warning, then?" asked Heathcliff, attempting a sneer. "Did she die like a saint? Come, give me a true history of the event. How did . . ." (p. 176).

The death of Cathy and its repercussions, however, do not end Nelly's failures that result from the great good fortune, for her own survival, of her native endowments. There remain young Cathy and the sickly son of Isabella for her to fail to comprehend. Dealing with them, she reveals her unimpaired self-confidence. Suspecting that young Cathy is corresponding with Linton, rather than question Cathy as might seem her duty as a guardian, she automatically uses the method of trying all her household keys on Cathy's locked drawer:

. . . I emptied the whole contents into my apron, and took them with me to examine at leisure in my own chamber. . . .

Some of them struck me as singularly odd compounds of ardour and flatness; commencing in strong feeling, and concluding in the affected,

H

wordy way that a schoolboy might use to a fancied, incorporeal sweetheart.

Whether they satisfied Cathy, I don't know, but they appeared very worthless trash to me.

After turning over as many as I thought proper, I tied them in a handkerchief and set them aside, re-locking the vacant drawer (p. 238).

Catherine's agony on realizing that the letters have been discovered is great, but Nelly sympathizes with her not at all, since to her both the letters and their author are contemptible.

Still harsher is her treatment of Cathy after the revelation of the visits to Wuthering Heights:

"Now, Ellen, you have heard all; and I can't be prevented from going to Wuthering Heights, except by inflicting misery on two people—whereas, if you'll only not tell papa, my going need disturb the tranquillity of none. You'll not tell, will you? It will be very heartless if you do."

"I'll make up my mind on that point by to-morrow, Miss Catherine," I replied. "It requires some study; and so I'll leave you to your rest, and go think it over."

I thought it over aloud, in my master's presence; walking straight from her room to his, and relating the whole story, with the exception of her conversations with her cousin, and any mention of Hareton (p. 268).

Though Edgar, no doubt, should know of the activities of his daughter, Nelly's methods are shown first in her promise to Cathy to consider the problem (the easy and immediate way of "smoothing over" that difficulty), second, in her immediate and unreflective revelation to Edgar, and third, in her holding back from Edgar those items that might cause her some trouble with him. Most revelatory of all, of course, is the more than satisfied manner in which she narrates the whole episode to Lockwood.

One can also contrast the superficiality of Nelly's understanding even with that of young Cathy in two passages very close together (pp. 304 and 307). Cathy, now his daughter-in-law, says in the former,

"Mr. Heathcliff, *you* have *nobody* to love you; and, however miserable you make us, we shall still have the revenge of thinking that your cruelty arises from your greater misery! You *are* miserable, are you not? Lonely, like the devil, and envious like him? *Nobody* loves you—*nobody* will cry for you, when you die! I wouldn't be you!"

The realization of cruelty as the consequence of misery is beyond Nelly who had once explained his character as due to the evil example of Hindley. To emphasize Nelly's inability to understand, immediately after the passage just quoted, Emily Brontë has Heathcliff tell Nelly of his opening of Cathy's grave, and the reader is more than ever aware of the torments he has suffered, especially when he ends, "It was a strange way of killing, not by inches, but by fractions of hairbreadths, to beguile me with the spectre of a hope, through eighteen years." To this she comments to Lockwood:

  Mr. Heathcliff paused and wiped his forehead—his hair clung to it, wet with perspiration; his eyes were fixed on the red embers of the fire; the brows not contracted, but raised next the temples, diminishing the grim aspect of his countenance, but imparting a peculiar look of trouble, and a painful appearance of mental tension towards one absorbing subject. He only half addressed me, and I maintained silence—*I didn't like to hear him talk* [italics mine].

And while he had been talking, she had interrupted him with, " 'You were very wicked, Mr. Heathcliff!' I exclaimed; 'were you not ashamed to disturb the dead?' " (p. 305), quick to register conventional horror at a breach of custom, but apparently oblivious of the overwhelming torment that had caused the breach. Here, with particular intensity, the reader revolts from accepting the wholesome, normal person as a criterion of thought and behaviour, and tends to accept any passion so long as it is real, and in so doing becomes his own active interpreter of the true state of affairs and is powerfully affected by the genuine insight into human emotion.

  Yet he may not be allowed to forget that Nelly is a fine

woman nevertheless; she is once more contrasted with Joseph when Lockwood finds both of them together on his unexpected visit in September 1802, just after, furthermore, he had encountered her cloddish successor at the Grange (see p. 324):

> . . . at the door, sat my old friend, Nelly Dean, sewing and singing a song, which was often interrupted from within, by harsh words of scorn and intolerance, uttered in far from musical accents.
>
> "Aw'd rayther, by the haulf, hev 'em swearing i' my lugs frough morn tuh neeght, nur hearken yah, hahsiver!" said the tenant of the kitchen, in answer to an unheard speech of Nelly's. "It's a blazing shaime, ut Aw cannut oppen t' Blessed Book, bud yah set up them glories tuh sattan, un' all t' flaysome wickednesses ut iver wer born intuh t' warld. . . . O Lord, judge 'em fur they's norther law nur justice amang wer rullers!"
>
> "No! Or we should be sitting in flaming fagots, I suppose," retorted the singer. "But wisht, old man, and read your Bible like a christian, and never mind me. This is 'Fairy Annie's Wedding'—a bonny tune—it goes to a dance" (pp. 326–327).

With this picture of Nelly's natural attractiveness and gaiety in mind we reach her narration of Heathcliff's end, his "queer" end, as she calls it (p. 328).

As any reader of the novel will have guessed, Nelly was taken by surprise at Heathcliff's death: as with all the other now dead characters, she had supposed him sound in all ways:

> "But what do you mean by a *change*, Mr. Heathcliff?" I said, alarmed at his manner, though he was neither in danger of losing his senses, nor dying; according to my judgment he was quite strong and healthy; and, as to his reason, from childhood, he had a delight in dwelling on dark things, and entertaining odd fancies. He might have had a monomania on the subject of his departed idol; but on every point his wits were as sound as mine (p. 344).

Such phrases as "delight in dwelling on dark things," "monomania on the subject of his idol!" are perhaps a climax in Nelly's brushing aside of all powerful emotion, and above all, it should be noted that the only thing that here alarms her is Heathcliff's unwholesome manner.

As his death approaches, Nelly finally begins to worry about him; she fears for a short time, as the only way of explaining him, that he must be some "ghoul, or a vampire" (p. 350), but rejects that explanation and tries to conjure up some type of parentage that would account for his nature, but concludes by turning her attention aside to a serious abnormality, that he will not be able to have a proper tombstone, since his age and true name are unknown: "We were obliged to content ourselves with the single word, 'Heathcliff.' . . . If you enter the kirk-yard, you'll head on his headstone, only that, and the date of his death" (p. 350). Her final words show how well for her own tranquillity she has settled the whole violent tale, when in response to Lockwood's half jest that the ghosts of Cathy and Heathcliff will be the future inhabitants of Wuthering Heights, " 'No, Mr. Lockwood,' said Nelly, shaking her head. 'I believe the dead are at peace, but it is not right to speak of them with levity' " (p. 358).

We have received the story almost entirely from Nelly, a representative of an admirable type of person, a character developed in great detail and with great skill, no obvious technical device, but a genuinely memorable character. In the circumstances in which she had been forced to live, she has revealed the futility of a tolerant, common-sense attitude which is the result of a desire merely to avoid trouble, to deny serious problems, and of a failure to grasp genuinely the emotions of others; the futility of compromise which is a mere improvisation from day to day in the interest of averting "explosions," of the futility of a constant attempt to preserve surface decorum and tranquillity on the grounds that what does not appear will not do any harm, and she has made the reader feel that her action has been throughout the best that can be expected of the type she represents. The reader continually decreases in sympathy with a type that he would usually admire, as she goes healthily and happily singing about her household duties and amusing the babies, since her so consistently emphasized good qualities turn out to be of so little use.

Thus, constantly rejecting her explanations, the reader substitutes his own, based always on the available evidence which she supplies but does not take into account or understand, and he becomes through his own perceptions increasingly sympathetic with the thoughts, feelings, and deeds of Heathcliff and Cathy.

The engaging of the reader actively as one who does a large part of the work of comprehending is an important cause of the power of the novel. As Nelly contentedly provides her superficial interpretations of motive, and contentedly recounts her inadequate parental behaviour, we are constantly directed towards feeling the inadequacy of the wholesome, and towards sympathy with genuine passions, no matter how destructive or violent.

The Narrator in
"Wuthering Heights"*

BONAMY DOBRÉE

I T IS universally acknowledged that *Wuthering Heights* is a great work of art, in itself an experience : it colours our view of what life is about. It is of enormous interest to ask ourselves, not "How did this astonishing thing happen?"—one cannot track down genius in that way—but rather "By what means did Emily Brontë produce her effect?" We may be quite sure that this is not the lucky result of untutored genius flinging itself haphazard at the task. The actors live in as small an enclosed world as they do in any of Ibsen's later plays, and the book has all the tension of a drama, together with the final effect of drama rather than of the novel : that is, we do not drop into a muse when we have finished it : we feel exhilaration. This is the achieved result of long brooding on the theme until the imagination encounters the symbols which will embody it : and then of the imagination concentrating powerfully on the means of making these living symbols real for other people. That is where the intellectual problem must emerge with the intuitional creation.

Emily Brontë had had practice in the Gondal romance or

* Reprinted, with the kind permission of the publishers, from the introduction to the Collins Classics edition of "Wuthering Heights" (1953, 1964).

epic, and in the other writings conducted by all four Brontë children; so there is nothing slack or amateurish about the conception of this book. The relationships of the people, the working out of the dates of the events, the fitting in of the various conflicts, all are mechanically perfect; and what is more, Emily Brontë had learnt, so that she might apply it here, the complicated law of inheritance which prevailed, not when she wrote, but at the time of the story she was telling. She must, we see, have been able to live in a vivid state of actuality with her people while she was creating them. Not that this is uncommon, for after all, this is what normally constitutes inspiration; what is rare is the faculty of intense visual imagination which she shared with her elder sister, a sense of vision so strong that she can impart it to us incidentally, almost: she never has to reassure herself of the existence of her people by describing them minutely.

What may seem nearly as astonishing when considering a first novel, written before much had been said about the craft of fiction, is that Emily Brontë seems to have been acutely alive to the problem of presenting her material, of making her vision tell upon the page. She must certainly have pondered the technical side of novel writing, and it surely was deliberately that she chose the two narrators as vehicles for her tale. It might have been better, we may think, if she had taken up the position of the all-seeing creator, the method usually adopted by her predecessors and contemporaries when they were not using the autobiographical convention clearly unsuitable here : but whereas the omniscient method is well enough where there is no temptation to disbelieve what you are told, as, say, in Jane Austen's novels which deal with the normal, here, with so wild a story, the method would have exposed its greatest flaw, namely that there is nothing to guarantee for the reader that he is being told the truth. Yet it was essential to Emily Brontë's

purpose that you should believe it, wholly and utterly accept it:
so she gave the story into the hands of two narrators, each of
whom can say, "This is true; I was there; this is what happened." We know then that the story is authentic.

But how was Emily Brontë to find someone who would
always be, who could plausibly be, there, just when it was
absolutely necessary for her to be present? She had recourse to
the confidential servant, brought up with the children of the
family, necessarily involved in all their affairs. But then, how
can an uneducated woman have the knowledge—of complex
circumstances, of outrageous sentiments, of words, of artful
story-telling—to satisfy the requirements of a story at that level,
to be a trustworthy witness? Emily Brontë was quite aware of
the difficulty: almost as soon as Ellen Dean begins to take up
the tale, she reassures her temporary master: "I have under-
gone sharp discipline, which has taught me wisdom: and then,
I have read more than you would fancy, Mr. Lockwood. . . ."
question or to care. It is true, on examination, that only a very
highly cultured, literary woman, could speak and discuss as
Nelly does at the end of the book: but by that time verisimilitude has ceased to matter—to anyone for whom the means of
communication offered by novels has any validity at all.

Yet—a further complication, which might have been disastrous—it is not to us, but to Lockwood, that she tells her story.
Lockwood even repeats to us what Nelly says somebody else
told her was uttered by yet another person, as when we know
what the Lintons remarked when the Wuthering Heights children broke in upon them. All their sayings are reported verbatim, and this undoubtedly introduces a certain clumsiness.
Every method involves its own risks, exacts even some payment: the question is, can the author, by proper handling of
the method, keep up so great a pressure on our consciousness,
We too are at the moment reassured: and soon we cease to

our recipience, as to justify the price paid in verisimilitude? It must be confessed that once or twice, in the very middle of the book, our belief wavers. What, we ask, was the "good authority" which apprised Dr. Kenneth of there being something afoot between Heathcliff and Isabella? And how, soon afterwards, did Nelly Dean get Isabella's letter, and why was such an unlikely epistle addressed to her at all? Just for a moment, then, the pressure slackens: but it is for a moment only that we feel uneasiness. Such is the force and passion of the prose, the speed of the narrative, that we soon accept again.

For though the story seems thus unnecessarily involved, it does not seem so in the reading, for the scenes are dramatized without our noticing it; the "he said"s are left out whenever dramatic actuality is demanded. Moreover Nelly is introduced as narrator only after we have had what is, so to speak, a first-hand glimpse of the atrocious agony of feeling which gives the book its power. For the deep emotions in action are presented to us, not in retrospect as they ultimately must be with a narrator, but as a violent scene in which the first narrator, Lockwood, is willy-nilly caught up. We do not have to wait for Nelly and her contemporaries, Cathy and Hindley and Heathcliff to become responsible adults, but are plunged straightway into the maelstrom of feelings which direct the story. Today the method is the ordinary one—it was not so much the routine in 1846—a scene to begin with, then a retrospect, then a summary, with the tale going on: even so, in this book, the first scene is very long, and the retrospect occupies nearly all the rest of the book: the summary and the continuing tale are almost in the nature of an epilogue. All the same the effect is achieved.

Nelly is brilliantly thought out and executed; nothing more clearly reveals the power of a novelist than making the vehicle of communication really convey the intuition, and not merely relate events. Since she is the confidante of so many people, the

story does not suffer from the usual defect of the narrator
method, that of seeing people from only one point of view:
Heathcliff, for example, we see not only through her eyes, but
through the first Catherine's, when she tells Isabella what
Heathcliff is like; through the unlucky Linton Heathcliff's,
when Nelly sees him shrink in terror from his father; and even
through the devoted eyes (an amazing touch of art) of Hareton
Earnshaw. Lockwood too is admirably conceived as a narrator;
he never has to be drawn into the emotional development; he is
external and detached, though he is not unnecessary to the story.
For he is all unconsciously an agent, and we realize at the end
that it was his visitation by the ghost of Cathy (if we choose to
regard his nightmare as such) that precipitated Heathcliff's final
crisis. Apart from that, however, he is outside the story. His
role is to add convincing evidence to what Nelly tells us through
him, since he has no need to lie, no subconscious urge to conceal,
reveal, or justify. He clinches Nelly's statements: he confirms
for us the ghastly truth of what she tells. It is through this quite
disinterested person that from the very beginning we feel the
tension of the whole story.

So much for what we might call the purely mechanical side;
there is more to be noticed. We see that since Nelly is so often
"there" we do not miss any of the dramatic possibilities when
the great scenes occur, but we have to realize further that this
can happen only because she is the kind of person Emily Brontë
chose to make her. It is not simply that as a family servant she
identifies herself with the family and is personally involved in
all that happens: it is that her own feelings are part of the
drama; it is through her passion that we feel it. One might instance this particularly from her anger with Cathy at her fatal
fit of temper when Heathcliff is turned out of Thrushcross.
Moreover, she has enough of the peasant in her to be able to sit
and brood over the past; she re-lives it, one feels, over and over

again; it is all arranged (or re-arranged) in her mind with perfect clarity. So that when she tells any part of the story she does
actually re-live it, and the drama is vividly present to her, not
dimly seen, not sophisticated, as it nearly always is in a narrator's retrospect. Again, for Emily Brontë's purpose, she is just
educated enough to understand what is happening, but not so
educated as to be anything but acceptant. There is no scepticism
in her. Someone more analytical could not have told about
Heathcliff's last visionary days, if only, for one thing, that
Heathcliff could not have talked as he did to any other kind of
person.

Nelly, then, is not a mere mechanical vehicle; she is part of
the emotional texture, not simply chorus to the tragic scene in
company with the hideous Joseph. She is there at every one of
the crucial moments except the tremendous opening one where
Lockwood sees Heathcliff frantically imploring Cathy's ghost
to come in. It is to her that Cathy says: "I *am* Heathcliff"; it is
to her that Heathcliff says: "My soul's bliss kills my body, but
doesn't satisfy itself." It is she who is present at the last despairing interview between the two eternal lovers, where at once
both Heaven seems to open and Hell to gape. Nevertheless all
the time Emily Brontë is in control—perhaps Ellen Dean was
her sheet anchor in this respect. But then she can be broken
away from. Lockwood, the detached—or almost detached—
observer comes back to report to us directly; and how ingeni-
ously, we note, Emily Brontë had sent him away for a few
months, so that Nelly can tell him the rest of the story quickly.
The tale thus gathers speed towards the end, and the gap en-
ables a sane love, not the "monomania" of Heathcliff or the tormented possession of the elder Catherine, to break in upon the
fire-purged horror, so that the story can be dovetailed, as it were,
into our daily life lived at the normal intensity.

Without this end, and the concluding words which seem—

though on analysis rather uncertainly—to bring a kind of pagan peace to this utterly pagan and deeply religious tragedy, the whole might be unendurable. As it is it has a strange magnificence, though what the magnificence resides in cannot be defined neatly; it is partly in the form which itself conveys the intuition. Nor can we readily lay our finger on what precisely the evil is, or what distorted the good to make it evil. The tragic reconciliation is perhaps not fully expressed, and its final statement is to be found rather in the Gondal poems, more particularly we might say in the famous "No coward soul is mine," written early in the year when *Wuthering Heights* took shape in words, a poem in which the sense prevails that all prisoned souls, such as Heathcliff and Catherine felt themselves to be, finally exist in the One. In the meantime there are Hareton and the younger Catherine. Ordinary life must still be lived, as wholesomely as may be.

Charlotte Brontë
as a Critic of
"Wuthering Heights"*

PHILIP DREW

> *The faults of* Wuthering Heights *proceed,
> not from defective knowledge of human
> nature, but from inferior technique, from an
> insufficient acquaintance with the craft of
> fiction. The story is in general ill constructed,
> and in its detail often complicated and ob-
> scure. In parts it is uncertainly conceived, the
> pattern of it haunted by bad example—the
> "novel of edification" and the "Tale of
> Terror" both lend to it vicious elements.*†

EMILY BRONTË's technique has not lacked defenders in
recent years;[1] one may feel that Garrod's objections have been
answered in full and that in addition there is now general recognition of the positive virtues of Emily Brontë's style and of the
powerful effects of her complex system of narration and of her

---

* © 1964 by The Regents of the University of California. Reprinted from *Nineteenth-Century Fiction*, volume XVIII, pp. 365–381.

† H. W. Garrod, Introduction to World's Classics edition.

[1] For example, *The Structure of Wuthering Heights*, by C. P. S(anger), (*Hogarth
Essays*, XIX); David Cecil in *Early Victorian Novelists* (1934); D. Traversi (*Dublin
Review*, CCXXII); J. K. Mathison (*NCF*, XI); Carl Woodring (*NCF*, XI); Miriam
Allott (*Essays in Criticism*, VIII).

peculiarly tightly-woven plot, economizing in characters, dispensing with them ruthlessly as soon as they have served their purpose by bearing a child, and generally concentrating the story to a few personages in a single place. The most obvious example of the care with which Emily Brontë works is the ironic correspondence between the two halves of the novel. The younger Catherine, Hareton, and Linton re-enact the parts of Cathy, Heathcliff, and Edgar at Heathcliff's bidding. Catherine's marriage to the sickly and malicious Linton is Heathcliff's bitter caricature of Cathy's marriage to Edgar. This is why the idea of Cathy's ghost is so plausible: in a sense her life is being lived over again.

The effect of this critical preoccupation with Miss Brontë's technique has been to withdraw attention from a direct consideration of the moral implications of the book, although clearly such a consideration is necessary for a judgment of its success or failure, especially of Heathcliff's fitness to stand as the central figure.[2]

Of the critics who comment explicitly on the book's subject and its moral import one of the earliest is Charlotte Brontë. Although her critical powers are disabled by Garrod, the points she makes in her preface to the edition of 1850 are so different from those which trouble modern critics that they are worth careful attention on their own account, to say nothing of their unique value as the comments of an intelligent and informed contemporary, who was peculiarly well placed to understand the nature of the authoress's achievement.

At the beginning of her preface, Charlotte Brontë apologizes ironically to those too delicately brought up to enjoy the story of unpolished moorland people and to those who are offended by seeing words (presumably "damn," "devil," and "hell") written out in full. She continues by apologizing in the same

[2] Mrs. Allott's article is a notable exception.

vein for the rusticity of *Wuthering Heights*, although she is in fact defending it as authentic and inevitable.

> With regard to the rusticity of *Wuthering Heights*, I admit the charge, for I feel the quality. It is rustic all through. It is moorish, and wild, and knotty as the root of heath. Nor was it natural that it should be otherwise; the author being herself a native and nursling of the moors. . . . Had Ellis Bell been a lady or a gentleman accustomed to what is called "the world," her view of a remote and unreclaimed region, as well as of the dwellers therein, would have differed greatly from that actually taken by the homebred country girl. Doubtless it would have been wider—more comprehensive : whether it would have been more original or more truthful is not so certain.

This point established, she explains how Emily became obsessed with the more "tragic and terrible traits" of Yorkshire life, and how her character was such that she could not understand why anyone should object to the depiction of scenes so vivid and so fearful. Charlotte's next step is to discuss the characters of the book in the light of her knowledge of her sister's imagination and of the atmosphere of the Yorkshire moors : it is here that she is most at variance with modern criticism.

She begins, "For a specimen of true benevolence and homely fidelity, look at the character of Nelly Dean." A feature of recent criticism of the book has been the suggestion that Nelly is far from an adequate character—that Emily Brontë wishes us to set her uncultivated, undemanding, homespun, conventional morality in unfavourable contrast to the passion of Heathcliff and the elder Catherine.[3] In support of this, one may observe that she plays a crucial part in the action and that this part is often weak and temporizing. So that Nelly-as-actor often annoys us and disposes us to distrust and even to resist the explicit judgments of Mrs. Dean-as-narrator. There are three reasons for supposing that this is not a deliberate effect con-

---

[3] For example, by Garrod (Introduction to World's Classics edition, p. x), and by J. K. Mathison (*op. cit.*).

trived by Emily Brontë to cast doubt on Mrs. Dean's value as a
source of moral standards. First, she is honest about her own
failures, admitting her errors of judgment and her compla-
cency; in fact she so often reflects ironically on her own inade-
quacies that James Hafley is able to suggest, in a most entertain-
ing article,[4] that she is the villain of the book. Second, many of
the foolish things she does are required by the necessities of the
plot, and are more accurately seen as clumsiness or obviousness
of contrivance than as deliberate devices to discredit her. Third,
Lockwood is already set up as the source of conventional urban
judgments and Joseph as the source of narrow moral judgments. If we must choose either Mrs. Dean's morality or Heathcliff's, there is no doubt which we are to prefer. Nelly Dean is
of the moors; Heathcliff is an incomer. She is shown to be fairly
perceptive, kindly, loyal, and, in particular, tolerant. Thus she
finds many good things to say about Heathcliff, but on balance
she feels bound to condemn him. Since we see the story through
her eyes and she is not presented ironically, her verdict carries
great weight with the reader. But for her the book would hardly
have any point of normal reference. Isabella uses a significant
phrase in her letter to Nelly in Chapter XIII, "How did you
contrive to preserve the common sympathies of human nature
when you resided here?"

Charlotte's preface continues, "For an example of constancy
and tenderness, remark [the character] of Edgar Linton." This
view of Edgar is more favourable than that of most modern
critics, who generally regard him as "a poor creature,"[5] but
there is good warrant for it in the novel. For example, in Chapter XVIII Nelly describes Linton's demeanour after Catherine's
death: ". . . . he was too good to be thoroughly unhappy long.
He didn't pray for Catherine's soul to haunt him. Time brought

---

[4] *NCF*, XIII (Dec., 1958).   [5] Cecil.

I

resignation and a melancholy sweeter than common joy. He recalled her memory with ardent, tender love, and hopeful aspiring to the better world, where he doubted not she was gone." A
little later she contrasts him favourably with Hindley: "Linton . . . displayed the true courage of a loyal and faithful soul.
He trusted God, and God comforted him. One hoped, and the
other despaired. They chose their own lots, and were righteously
doomed to endure them." I find it impossible to believe that
Emily Brontë intended either of those passages to be read as
ironical.

Charlotte Brontë's comments on Joseph and young Catherine
are unremarkable, but of the older Catherine she has this to
say: "Nor is even the first heroine of the name destitute of a
certain strange beauty in her fierceness, or of honesty in the
midst of perverted passion and passionate perversity." This surprising judgment must be considered in conjunction with Charlotte Brontë's verdict on Heathcliff, which may be summed up
by the beginning of its first sentence: "Heathcliff, indeed,
stands unredeemed; never once swerving in his arrow-straight
course to perdition."

This is the crucial point in her criticism of the novel. Her
assessment of Heathcliff depends on a recognition of his superhuman villainy, whereas modern critics, if they move away from
a consideration of the book's mechanism to a consideration of
the moral relations of the characters, usually choose to mini-
mize or justify Heathcliff's consistent delight in malice in order
to elevate him to the status of hero. An article by E. F. Shannon
(*NCF*, Sept., 1959) represents this kind of criticism at its strongest. In the course of his article, Shannon says, "Within the
ethical context of the novel, he [Heathcliff] is paradoxically
accurate when, near death, he replies to Nelly's exhortation to
penitence 'As to repenting of my injustices, I've done no injustice, and I repent of nothing.'" To decide between these con-

flicting views, the first step is to see whether or not Charlotte
bases her judgment on an accurate description of Heathcliff's
conduct in the course of the novel.

In the early part of the book, we are led to suspect him of
nothing worse than a hot temper, a proud nature, and a capacity
for implacable hatred. Indeed until he is sixteen the balance of
sympathy is with him, since he has been treated so ill. The worst
that Nelly says of him is, ". . . without having bad features, or
being deficient in intellect, he contrived to convey an impression
of inward and outward repulsiveness that his present aspect re-
tains no traces of" (Chapter VIII). But all this (except perhaps
the word "inward") could be laid at the door of Hindley's cruel
treatment of him.

However, when he returns after three years' absence to find
Catherine married to Edgar, it is clear that his character has
changed. Catherine herself says (Chapter X) "He's a fierce,
pitiless, woolfish man," and Nelly confirms that he is leading
Hindley to perdition. The remarkable thing about this is that
Heathcliff has been back at Wuthering Heights for at most four
months (September, 1783–January, 1784) and has not yet quar-
relled with Catherine: yet she describes his nature so.

He courts Isabella not so much for her property as for revenge
on Edgar. That he does not love her he makes plain in Chapter
X, when he says of her, "You'd hear of odd things if I lived
alone with that mawkish waxen face. The most ordinary would
be painting on its white the colours of the rainbow, and turning
the blue eyes black, every day or two." Later Catherine says to
him, "I won't repeat my offer of a wife. It is as bad as offering
Satan a lost soul. Your bliss lies, like his, in inflicting misery"
(Chapter XI). She goes on to say that Heathcliff is destroying
her happiness with Edgar: his conduct in the succeeding chapters bears this out. He runs off with Isabella through malice,
despising her as he does so, and before he leaves, hangs her pet

spaniel. He says himself, "The first thing she saw me do on coming out of the Grange was to hang up her little dog, and when she pleaded for it, the first words I uttered were a wish that I had the hanging of every being belonging to her, except one." Isabella writes of him, "He is ingenious and unresting in seeking to gain my abhorrence. I sometimes wonder at him with an intensity that deadens my fear; yet I assure you a tiger or a venomous serpent could not rouse terror in me equal to that which he wakens" (Chapter XIII). It may be held that Isabella is not an impartial witness : the point is that her letter, written a bare two months after marriage, expresses nothing but bitter hatred of her husband, and is itself testimony to his treatment of her. Of this treatment Heathcliff says, "I've sometimes relented, from pure lack of invention, in my experiments on what she could endure and still creep shamefully cringing back" (Chapter XIV). Later in the same chapter he says, "I have no pity! I have no pity! The more the worms writhe, the more I yearn to crush out their entrails! It is a moral teething; and I grind with greater energy in proportion to the increase of pain."

Even in his grief for Cathy's death he still behaves cruelly to Isabella; when she had fled from Wuthering Heights after Heathcliff has thrown a dinner-knife at her, she remarks temperately, "Catherine had awfully perverted taste to esteem him so dearly, knowing him so well." Heathcliff must also fall under strong suspicion of murdering Hindley Earnshaw, whom he has already ruined and driven to the brink of madness. He has also knocked him down and kicked him in the course of a quarrel. Nelly asks herself, "Had he [Hindley] fair play?" and Joseph implies that when he set off for the doctor Hindley was far from dead. Heathcliff says that Hindley was "both dead and cold and stark" before the doctor came, but this must be wrong, since Kenneth reached Thrushcross with the news while it was still early morning (Chapter XVII). Nelly com-

ments on Heathcliff's bearing after Hindley's death, "He maintained a hard, careless deportment, indicative of neither joy nor
sorrow; if anything, it expressed a flinty gratification at a piece
of difficult work successfully executed." Thus, having ruined
Hindley and made himself master of Wuthering Heights and
of young Hareton, and having driven away Isabella and his
own child, Heathcliff has completed the first stage of his revenge, much of it during the lifetime of the elder Catherine.

There is then a gap of twelve years while the younger generation grows up. During this time, Heathcliff carries out his plan
to degrade and pervert Hareton. Later he insists on possession
of his son, Linton, and treats him with notable callousness.
Finally he lays his plans to trap the younger Catherine into
marriage with his son, first prompting Linton into a correspondence with her, and then telling her that Linton is dying for love
of her. He uses his son, who is close to death, simply as a bait
for Catherine, not because she will have money (all she will
bring Linton is what Edgar has set aside for her, although this
is referred to as a "fortune"), but to make her wretched. When
Linton is very ill, Heathcliff compels him by terror to lure
Catherine into Wuthering Heights. "What was filling him with
dread we had no means of discerning; but there he was, powerless under its gripe, and any addition seemed capable of shocking him into idiocy." When they are in the house and the door
is locked, Heathcliff says of Linton and Catherine, "It's odd
what a savage feeling I have to anything that seems afraid of
me. Had I been born where laws are less strict and tastes less
dainty, I should treat myself to a slow vivisection of these two
as an evening's amusement" (Chapter XXVII). He seizes Catherine and administers "a shower of terrific slaps on both sides of
the head"; he then imprisons her for four or five days, although
her father is on his deathbed. "Miss Linton, I shall enjoy myself
remarkably in thinking your father will be miserable; I shall

not sleep for satisfaction." He thus forces her to marry his son (exactly how this was done is not made clear) and then sets him against her : he knocks Catherine down and takes her locket. After Catherine's escape he punishes Linton.

"I brought him down one evening, the day before yesterday, and just set him in a chair, and never touched him afterwards. I sent Hareton out, and we had the room to ourselves. In two hours I called Joseph to carry him up again; and, since then, my presence is as potent on his nerves as a ghost; and I fancy he sees me often, though I am not near. Hareton says he wakes and shrieks in the night by the hour together . . ." (Chapter XXIX).

When Linton is dying, Heathcliff refuses to send for the doctor ("His life is not worth a farthing, and I won't spend a farthing on him"), and his son dies. When Heathcliff is himself on the point of death, he says, "As to repenting of my injustices, I've done no injustice, and I repent of nothing" (Chapter XXXIV).

His whole career from the time of his return (September, 1783) to his death (May, 1802) is one of calculated malice : during this time he does not perform one single good or kindly action,[6] and continually expresses his hatred of all the other characters. So extreme is his malevolence indeed that one might expect him to impress critics as a grotesque villain, like Quilp in *The Old Curiosity Shop*. But this is far from the case. Melvin R. Watson's article on *"Wuthering Heights* and the Critics" (*NCF*, March, 1949) provides a convenient conspectus. He speaks approvingly of the opinion of Mrs. Robinson : "She insists rightly that Heathcliff is the central figure and that he harms no one seriously who had not either harmed him or asked for trouble." One can see that this is simply an inaccurate account of the novel, but as Watson's article shows, it may fairly be taken as representative of much recent criticism of

---

[6] But notice that E. F. Shannon (*op. cit.*) makes the following point in Heathcliff's favour: "Although a reluctant host, he provides Lockwood with a glass of wine, tea and dinner on separate occasions; and during the narrator's illness he sends him a brace of grouse and chats amiably at his 'bedside a good hour.' "

Wuthering Heights. How are we to account for the fact that, although Charlotte Brontë describes Heathcliff's conduct accurately, her judgment of his character has commanded virtually no support from later writers, and the very transactions on which this judgment is based are ignored? Why, in short, have critics responded so readily to Heathcliff as the hero of the novel and paid so little attention to his more conspicuous qualifications to be considered the villain?

Most obviously, the characters set in opposition to him are gentle to the point of weakness. Isabella, the younger Catherine and his own son are powerless to resist him, Hindley seems a frail old man, Edgar is not a man of action, and Nelly herself, who is Heathcliff's most persistent opponent, often behaves foolishly at vital points in the action. The reader is thus tempted to admire Heathcliff, as the Romantic critics admire Satan, for his energy and decisiveness, even his ruthlessness. A closer parallel to this attitude to Heathcliff may be found in *Sanditon*, where Sir Edward Denham speaks approvingly of "the high-toned machinations of the prime character, the potent pervading Hero of the Story," and contrasts them with "the tranquil and morbid virtues of any opposing characters." Of course Jane Austen is here satirizing Sir Edward's modish taste for the extravagances of the Gothic novel. If we discount such highly-charged romantic views of the Hero, what is to be found in *Wuthering Heights* itself which may be supposed to influence the reader in Heathcliff's favour?

It is frequently argued that Heathcliff is redeemed by his passionate love for Catherine Earnshaw. This is Charlotte Brontë's comment:

. . . his love for Catherine . . . is a sentiment fierce and inhuman: a passion such as might boil and glow in the bad essence of some evil genius; a fire that might form the tormented centre—the ever-suffering soul of a magnate of the infernal world: and by its quenchless and ceaseless ravage effect the execution of the decree which dooms him to carry Hell with him wherever he wanders.

In the rest of this article, I shall hope to show that this is a literally accurate description of Heathcliff's passion for Catherine.

The facts as given by Mrs. Dean are these. When Catherine is fifteen and Heathcliff sixteen, he hears her say that it would degrade her to marry him. She has in fact already accepted Edgar Linton. Heathcliff leaves Wuthering Heights then for over three years: the implication is that he is in love with Catherine. Before she knows that he has left, Catherine makes an impassioned declaration of her feelings for him.

> "If all else perished and *he* remained *I* should still continue to be. And if all else remained, and he were annihilated, the universe would turn to a mighty stranger—I should not seem a part of it. My love for Linton is like the foliage in the woods; time will change it, I'm well aware, as winter changes the trees. My love for Heathcliff resembles the eternal rocks beneath—a source of little visible delight, but necessary. Nelly, I *am* Heathcliff."

This speech is a fine one; it is quoted *ad nauseum*, and part of its power is transferred to Heathcliff. He is supposed to reciprocate Catherine's selfless love for him and to be redeemed by it. In fact, he reveals to Nelly and Isabella the selfishness of his love for Catherine and of the means he uses to convince himself that he is actually behaving more nobly than Edgar. This is especially plain in Chapter XIV, and culminates in Heathcliff's derisive comment on Edgar, "It is not in him to be loved like me." Yet Catherine declares her love for Edgar: "I love the ground under his feet, and the air over his head, and everything he touches, and every word he says. I love all his looks, and all his actions, and him entirely and altogether." When Heathcliff leaves and stays away for three years, Catherine gives no sign that the universe seems empty to her. On the contrary, she marries Edgar Linton, and Nelly comments, "I believe I may assert that they were really in possession of deep and growing happiness." Or as Catherine puts it herself, "I begin to be secure and tranquil." Catherine dies when she is eighteen and Heathcliff nineteen. As adults they are together for barely a sixth of the novel: they meet seldom and when they do they usually quarrel, until finally Heathcliff is goaded into marrying Isabella.

There is no doubt that this bond between Catherine and Heathcliff is extraordinarily powerful, but it is not a *justifying* bond. To describe it as "a love that springs from an elemental and natural affinity between them" and to imply that they act as they do merely through a pardonable excess of love, which is the prime virtue, is to fail to recognize its nature. On Heathcliff's side at least, it is selfish, which should warn us not to confuse it with love; it expresses itself only through violence— notice, for example, the extraordinary series of descriptions of violent physical contact during and immediately after Heathcliff's last meeting with Catherine; their passion for each other is so compounded with jealousy, anger, and hatred that it brings them only unhappiness, anguish, and eventually death; it is described as the instrument of Catherine's damnation by Mrs. Dean when she says, "Well might Catherine deem that heaven would be a land of exile to her, unless with her mortal body she cast away her mortal character also." In short, while we must recognize that the forging and breaking of the bond between Catherine and Heathcliff provides the novel with all its motive energy, it is fallacious to argue that this proves that Emily Brontë condones Heathcliff's behaviour and does not expect the reader to condemn it. Charlotte's phrase "perverted passion and passionate perversity" is exact.

We must consider next the argument, as advanced by Cecil, for example, that it was not Emily Brontë's intention that the reader should condemn Heathcliff, since he dictates the whole course of the novel, brings his schemes to a successful conclusion, and dies happily. A bitter remark of the younger Catherine's is relevant here. In Chapter XXIX she says:

> "Mr. Heathcliff, *you* have *nobody* to love you; and however miserable you make us, we shall still have the revenge of thinking that your cruelty arises from your greater misery! You *are* miserable, are you not? Lonely, like the devil, and envious like him? *Nobody* loves you—*nobody* will cry for you when you die! I wouldn't be you!"

Later in the same chapter, Heathcliff himself admits, talking of the older Catherine,

> "She showed herself, as she often was in life, a devil to me! And, since then, sometimes more and sometimes less, I've been the sport of that intolerable torture—infernal!—keeping my nerves at such a stretch that, if they had not resembled catgut, they would long ago have relaxed to the feebleness of Linton's. . . . It racked me. I've often groaned aloud, till that old rascal Joseph no doubt believed that my conscience was playing the fiend inside of me. . . . It was a strange way of killing—not by inches, but by fractions of hairbreadths—to beguile me with the spectre of a hope through eighteen years!"

"Strange happiness," as Nelly says. At the end of the book, Heathcliff's domination over the other characters fails, and he finds himself unable to plan further degradation for Catherine and Hareton.

> "It is a poor conclusion, is it not?" he observed . . . "an absurd termination to my violent exertions? I get levers and mattocks to demolish the two houses, and train myself to be capable of working like Hercules, and when everything is ready and in my power I find the will to lift a slate of either roof has vanished! My old enemies have not beaten me. Now would be the precise time to revenge myself on their representatives. I could do it, and none could hinder me. But where is the use? I don't care for striking; I can't take the trouble to raise my hand. That sounds as if I had been labouring the whole time only to exhibit a fine trait of magnanimity. It is far from being the case. I have lost the faculty of enjoying their destruction, and I am too idle to destroy for nothing" (Chapter XXXIII).

This passage leads on at once to Heathcliff's death. It is clear that his thwarted love of and vain grief for Catherine became perverted into the sadistic desire for revenge which sustained him for so many years. As soon as cruelty lost its savour, he lost all that was keeping him alive. At the end of his life, Nelly reproaches him for his wickedness (Chapter XXXIV), and her remarks are clearly just. They accord precisely with the spirit of Charlotte Brontë's preface.

The only point which Charlotte urges in Heathcliff's favour is what she calls "his rudely confessed regard for Hareton Earnshaw—the young man whom he has ruined." There is a strong resemblance between Hareton and Heathcliff, for both were poor dependents—half servant, half adopted son. Heathcliff perceived the likeness at the time of Hindley's death. "Now, my bonny lad, you are *mine*! And we'll see if one tree won't grow as crooked as another with the same wind to twist it" (Chapter XVII). He takes full advantage of the position.

"I've a pleasure in him," he continued, reflecting aloud. "He has satisfied my expectations. If he were a born fool I should not enjoy it half so much. But he's no fool; and I can sympathize with all his feelings, having felt them myself. I know what he suffers now, for instance, exactly. It is merely a beginning of what he shall suffer though. And he'll never be able to emerge from his bathos of coarseness and ignorance. I've got him faster than his scoundrel of a father secured me, and lower, for he takes a pride in his brutishness. I've taught him to scorn everything extra-animal as silly and weak" (Chapter XXI).

The crucial difference is that Hareton does not allow his ill-treatment to make him bitter; he even acquires a kind of fondness for Heathcliff. But this tells in his favour, not Heathcliff's, for it shows that Heathcliff was not *necessarily* brutalized by his environment, but rather that Hindley's ill-treatment of him encouraged a vindictiveness which he later deliberately fostered.

These are the strongest arguments I have found in justification of Heathcliff's conduct, and, as I have shown, none of them is of sufficient force to avert the reader's natural censure of his consistent malice and cruelty. The problem therefore is to reconcile our condemnation of his behaviour with his dominant place in the novel and in the reader's sympathies. Clearly, our attitude to the main character of a work of fiction need not be one of moral approval (e.g., Macbeth, Giles Overreach, Tamburlaine, Giovanni, Beatrice-Joanna, Becky Sharp, Pincher Martin), but he must in some way act with the reader's understanding and sympathy. In the remainder of this article, I should like to suggest one way in which Emily Brontë powerfully develops the reader's feelings in Heathcliff's favour.

In the earlier chapters our sympathies go naturally to Heathcliff (i.e., Lockwood's narrative and the first part of Nelly Dean's story—up to Chapter IX) since he is seen only as the victim of ill-treatment. As Charlotte wrote to W. S. Williams,[7]

"[Heathcliff] exemplified the effects which a life of continued injustice and hard usage may produce on a naturally perverse, vindictive, and inexorable disposition. Carefully trained and kindly treated, the black gipsy-cub might possibly have been reared into a human being, but tyranny and ignorance made of him a mere demon."

Heathcliff vanishes for three years, and these years are wrapped in mystery. Lockwood makes some historically plausible conjectures about them. "Did he finish his education on the Continent, and come back a gentleman? Or did he get a sizar's place at college, or escape to America, and earn honours by drawing blood from his foster-country, or make a fortune more promptly on the English highways?" (Chapter X). Mrs. Dean has to admit that she does not know: all she can say is that between the ages of sixteen and nineteen Heathcliff converted himself from an ignorant penniless servant to a man with

---

[7] Letter to W. S. Williams, August 14, 1848, quoted by L. and E. M. Hanson, *The Four Brontës* (p. 260).

money and black whiskers, a man of whom Catherine says, "It would honour the first gentleman in the country to be his friend." The mystery remains throughout the book.

After Heathcliff's return, he dominates the other characters, but, although he is now strong and his enemies weak, his life is one of continual torment. His sufferings engage the reader's natural sympathies, the more so as he suffers in a particular way, and one that accounts for, even if it cannot excuse, his wickedness. For Emily Brontë implies very strongly that if Heathcliff during his absence has not in fact sold his soul to the devil, he has effectively done so. Every description of him reinforces this implication, starting from Nelly's first meeting with him on his return. He appears suddenly in a patch of shadow, startling her.

"I have waited here an hour," he resumed, while I continued staring; "and the whole of that time all round has been as still as death. I dared not enter. You do not know me? Look, I'm not a stranger!"

A ray fell on his features; the cheeks were sallow and half covered with black whiskers, the brows lowering, the eyes deep-set and singular. I remembered the eyes.

"What!" I cried, uncertain whether to regard him as a worldly visitor, and I raised my hands in amazement. "What! you come back? Is it really you? Is it?"

"Yes, Heathcliff," he replied. . . . "I want to have one word with her —your mistress. Go, and say some person from Gimmerton desires to see her."

"How will she take it?" I exclaimed. "What will she do? The surprise bewilders me. It will put her out of her head. And you *are* Heathcliff, but altered! Nay, there's no comprehending it. Have you been for a soldier?"

"Go and carry my message," he interrupted impatiently. "I'm in hell till you do" (Chapter X).

Thereafter, hardly a chapter passes without some indication that Heathcliff is suffering the torments of a lost soul; from the moment of his return he is referred to as "ghoulish," "a devil," "a goblin," "Judas," and "Satan." Edgar says that his presence is "a moral poison that would contaminate the most virtuous."

After his marriage Isabella writes to Nelly, "The second question I have great interest in; it is this—Is Mr Heathcliff a man? If so, is he mad? And if not, is he a devil?" Hindley calls Heathcliff "hellish" and "a fiend." "Fiend" or "fiendish" is applied to him some seven times thereafter. Hindley is a powerful instrument for stressing the damnation of Heathcliff. He says,

> "Am I to lose *all* without chance of retrieval? Is Hareton to be a beggar? Oh, damnation! I *will* have it back, and I'll have his gold too, and then his blood, and hell shall have his soul! It will be ten times blacker with that guest than ever it was before!"

Heathcliff himself makes a revealing comment when he learns of Catherine's illness. He says that if he were ever to lose her, if, for example, she forgot him completely, 'Two words would comprehend my future—*death* and *hell*; existence after losing her would be hell." Shortly afterwards Isabella introduces the other word commonly used to refer to Heathcliff—"diabolical." Heathcliff is described as "diabolical" or "devilish" no fewer than six times: some comment on his infernal powers is thus made virtually every time he appears. Heathcliff's own outbursts to Catherine have a similar effect.

> "Are you possessed with a devil," he pursued savagely, "to talk in that manner to me when you are dying? Do you reflect that all those words will be branded in my memory and eating deeper eternally after you have left me? You know you lie to say I have killed you; and, Catherine, you know that I could as soon forget you as my existence! Is it not sufficient for your infernal selfishness that, while you are at peace, I shall writhe in the torment of hell?"

Similarly, shortly afterwards:

> "Yes, you may kiss me, and cry, and wring out my kisses and tears; they'll blight you—they'll damn you. . . . So much the worse for me that I am strong. Do I want to live? What kind of living will it be, when you —O God! would *you* like to live with your soul in the grave?" (Chapter XV).

This idea of souls being separated from bodies and its extension into the idea of ghosts walking the earth because there is no peace for them in the grave are pervasive in the book, and do much to reinforce the suggestion that evil powers are abroad. Heathcliff is particularly given to a belief in ghosts (Chapter XXIX).

For the rest of the book, Heathcliff is referred to variously as "an incarnate goblin," "a monster," "not a human being," and "a hellish villain"; Isabella refers to his "kin beneath," and talks of Hell as "his right abode." She says to Hindley, "His mouth watered to tear you with his teeth, because he's only half man—not so much—and the rest fiend!" (Chapter XVII).

Other characters refer to him as a "devil" (twice) and "a goblin." Nelly wonders whether he is wholly human. "'Is he a ghoul or a vampire?' I mused. I had read of such hideous incarnate demons." He says of himself to Catherine, "To you I've made myself worse than the devil." All through his adult life he undergoes what he describes as "that intolerable torture—infernal!" He says to Nelly when he is near death, "Last night I was on the threshhold of hell," and when he dies Joseph exclaims, "Th' divil's harried off his soul."

This network of references and comment serves to mark out Heathcliff as a possessed soul. If the story were expressly narrated on a supernatural level, his career could be described by saying simply that he sells his soul to the devil in exchange for power, power over others, and specifically power to make himself fit to marry Catherine. When however he attempts to claim his share of the bargain he finds that the devil is, as always, a cheat. He has the power he asked for but loses Catherine herself. He is left simply with power, the exercise of which he finds necessary but intolerably painful. Thereafter, he is consumed inwardly by hell-fire and the knowledge of his own damnation.

This would be a metaphorical way of describing what in fact

happens. Heathcliff's personality begins to disintegrate when he allows himself to become obsessed by a physical passion for Catherine and deliberately fosters this passion to the point of mania. He sacrifices every other part of his personality to the satisfaction of his passion, until by its very violence it destroys its own object. Once Catherine has gone, Heathcliff is left with no possible emotions except those into which he can pervert his previous obsession with Catherine. He finds that he can demonstrate that he has feelings only by expressing them as cruelty. This brings him no happiness: on the contrary his power for wickedness *is* his punishment, rather than his prize, just as his passion for Catherine was not a blessing but a curse. In short, he is destroying himself throughout the book: each act of wanton brutality is a further maiming of himself. "Treachery and violence are spears pointed at both ends. They wound those who resort to them worse than their enemies" (Chapter XVII). Time moves swiftly on the moors, and senility sets in very early (Hindley is only twenty-seven at his death), but nobody else ages as fast as Heathcliff. Towards his death, he seems to be consuming his life ever more rapidly, as if the processes of nature had been accelerated by the fires within. He acts like a fiend incarnate, but his actions torture him as much as they torture his victims: they are a part, and the worst part, of the torments of the damned which Heathcliff suffers during his life. When he finds himself capable of a good act, even one so neutral as not persecuting Hareton and Catherine, it is as though his sentence had been at last worked out, and he dies almost joyfully.

The sympathy that we give to him is thus not the sort that we give to the noble tragic hero, nor is it the same as our reluctant admiration of a powerfully defiant villain like Vittoria. It is more nearly akin to the compassion we feel for those who are fated to work out their doom in torment and despair, characters such as Satan himself, Marlowe's Faustus and Mephistopheles, the Wandering Jew, Vanderdecken, or even Captain Ahab.[8] It does not lead us to approve of Heathcliff's actions or even to condone them. Emily Brontë's achievement is to arouse our sympathy for a lost soul while making it quite clear that his actions are damnable.

All this is comprehended in Charlotte's preface. She sees that Heathcliff is embarked on an "arrow-straight course to perdition," and that his love for Catherine is a fire "that might form the tormented centre—the ever-suffering soul of a magnate of the infernal world" doomed "to carry Hell with him wherever he wanders." She concludes her remarks on his character by saying that but for one or two slight redeeming features "we should say he was child neither of Lascar nor gipsy, but a man's shape animated by demon life—a Ghoul—an Afreet." She thus identifies the novel's main source of evil energy and its central metaphor, which is the parallel between diabolical possession and embittered passion. Her concluding paragraph expresses with some subtlety the extent of Emily Brontë's achievement in liberating this terrifying energy and yet controlling it.

Wuthering Heights was hewn in a wild workshop, with simple tools, out of homely materials. The statuary found a granite block on a solitary moor: gazing thereon, he saw how from the crag might be elicited a head, savage, swart, sinister; a form moulded with at least one element of grandeur—power. . . . With time and labour, the crag took human shape; and there it stands colossal, dark, and frowning, half statue, half rock: in the former sense, terrible and goblin-like; in the latter, almost beautiful, for its colouring is of mellow grey, and moorland moss clothes it; and heath, with its blooming bells and balmy fragrance, grows faithfully close to the giant's foot.

---

[8] Mrs. Allott (*op. cit.*) suggests that Heathcliff sometimes reminds us of Byron's Manfred or Cain. Muriel Spark and Derek Stanford (*Emily Brontë*, London, 1953) note this also, but as a major weakness in the drawing of Heathcliff who, they say, "is Byron in prose dress."

K

Infanticide and Sadism in "Wuthering Heights"*

WADE THOMPSON

THIS ARTICLE will offer an interpretation of *Wuthering Heights* based upon the extraordinary sadism which underlies Emily Brontë's concept of emotional relationships and indicate the significance of her preoccupation with infanticide. Unless one appreciates the importance of infanticide and sadism in *Wuthering Heights*, one cannot appreciate the nature of the love between Catherine and Heathcliff, a love which I believe to have been frequently misunderstood, nor can one understand the motivation behind Heathcliff's killing of his own son. My chief contention is that *Wuthering Heights* is basically a perverse book—I use the word without its usual pejorative connotations—and that its power is owing precisely to its perversity.

I

In the first place, we may note that the children in *Wuthering Heights*, like the children in the Brontë household, are left to fend for themselves early in life without the love or protection

* Reprinted by permission of the Modern Language Association from *PMLA*, vol. LXXVIII (1963).

of their mothers. Catherine Earnshaw is not quite eight when her mother dies; Cathy Linton's birth coincides with her mother's death; Hareton's mother dies in the year of his birth; and Heathcliff is an orphan by the time he is seven. Even the children who receive motherly care throughout their childhood do not receive it long after they reach puberty. Linton Heathcliff loses his mother when he is not quite thirteen—Linton, of course, is a child all his life—and Isabella Linton is orphaned when she is fourteen. The only exceptions—and these unimportant—are Hindley Earnshaw and Edgar Linton, who are sixteen and eighteen respectively when their mothers die (and even their mothers are apparently not very "motherly").[1]

Without the care of their mothers,[2] the children find themselves in a fierce struggle for survival against actively hostile adults who seem obsessed with the desire to kill or maim them. From Lockwood's early dream of pulling the wrist of the ghost-child Catherine along a jagged window ledge, to Heathcliff's presiding with delight over the death of his overgrown child, the novel plays a multitude of insistent variations on the ghastly theme of infanticide. When Heathcliff is brought as a boy to the Earnshaw home, Mrs. Earnshaw's first reaction is to "fling it out doors." That night even the fairly kind-hearted Nelly Dean[3]

---

[1] For dates and ages I am indebted to C. P. Sanger's classic essay, The Structure of *Wuthering Heights* (London, 1926).

[2] Throughout the novel the reader is given occasional reminders of the lack of motherly love. In the opening chapter, for example, the little puppies get magnificent protection from the huge bitch pointer—the kind of protection that children never get. And sprinkled metaphors carry the same reminder, e.g., "No mother could have nursed an only child more devotedly . . ." "Never did any bird flying back to a plundered nest which it had left brimful of chirping young ones, express more complete despair . . ."

[3] James Hafley argues that Nelly Dean is the arch-villain and that Heathcliff is a kind of Othello who never realizes her treachery. "The Villain in *Wuthering Heights*," NCF, XIII (1958), 199–215. This argument is absurdly overstated, but it does have the merit of pointing out the ruthlessness of Nelly Dean's stratagems and expediencies. The fact is, however, that Nelly Dean's villainy is the villainy of the corporal who wishes to become top-sergeant and is perfectly willing to manipulate officers in order to gain rank.

puts "it" on the landing in the hope that "it might be gone on the morrow." Later, old Mr. Linton apprehends "it" prowling about with Catherine near Thrushcross Grange and immediately proclaims, "It is but a boy . . . would it not be a kindness to the country to hang him at once . . .?" Isabella Linton puts this sentiment in her own childish terms: "Frightful thing! Put him in the cellar, papa."

The infant Hareton Earnshaw lives in much greater danger. Hindley's first instinct when drunk is to kill his son, whom Nelly Dean constantly hides. At one time Heathcliff accidentally rescues Hareton from a fall, but is so incensed by the mistake that "had it been dark . . . he would have tried to remedy the mistake by smashing Hareton's skull on the steps." Later Heathcliff is possessed by an irrepressible desire to "twist" the life of Hareton: "We'll see if one tree won't grow as crooked as another," he says, and Nelly Dean thinks that Hareton's natural "soil" might have yielded "luxuriant crops" without such deliberate stunting.

Hareton manages somehow to survive, but Linton Heathcliff is slowly tortured to death by his father, whose desire to kill him is overwhelming: "Had I been born where laws are less strict and tastes less dainty, I should treat myself to a slow vivisection of those two [Linton and Cathy] as an evening's amusement."

Even at Thrushcross Grange, where the children do not have to hold their breaths for fear of being killed, the solicitude for their welfare is erratic and motherly feelings not very strong. Cathy is an "unwelcome" child, "neglected" at birth, who "might have wailed out of life, and nobody cared a morsel, during those first hours of existence." Isabella, even as an expectant mother, apparently does not like children and orders Nelly to "put poor Catherine's baby away: I don't like to see it!" So too Edgar Linton, despite his consistently loving care, is willing to entertain the thought of killing his daughter rather than let her marry Linton: "I'd rather resign her to God, and lay her in the earth before me," he says.

The infanticide theme is amplified symbolically throughout the novel in the killing of helpless and delicate animals. Early in the story Lockwood finds a heap of dead rabbits in the Heathcliff household. On one occasion, Isabella knocks over Hareton, "who was hanging a litter of puppies from a chair-back." Heathcliff shows Isabella what kind of man he is by hanging her little pet springer. In her death-bed delirium, Catherine recalls how she and Heathcliff saw a lapwing's nest "full of little skeletons. Heathcliff set a trap over it, and the old ones dare not come." Linton Heathcliff's favourite sport is to torture to death cats whose claws and teeth have been pulled.

The killing of helpless animals forms the basis of numerous metaphors. Thus Edgar Linton could no more leave Catherine than a cat could "leave a mouse half killed, or a bird half eaten." Isabella in Heathcliff's hands is like "a little canary in the park on a winter's day." Or again, Hindley Earnshaw is like a "stray sheep" which "God had forsaken," and Heathcliff is "an evil beast" which "prowled between it and the fold."

Directly and indirectly, then, Emily Brontë envisions a world in which the young and the weak live in constant peril. How compelling this vision was to the author may be indicated by the persistence of the infanticide motif in her poetry. The poem beginning, " 'Twas night; her comrades gathered all," records a particularly gruesome act of child-murder:

> "Say, sin shall never blanch that cheek
> Nor suffering charge that brow;
> Speak, in thy mercy, Maker, speak,
> And seal it safe from woe!"

At this point the speaker realizes her mission.

> "Why did I doubt? In God's control
> Our mutual fates remain;
> And pure as now my angel's soul
> *Must* go to Heaven again."

Another poem, beginning "I've seen this dell in July's shine,"
records a mother's yearning for summer, because "July's shine"
would make ideal weather for killing her child. As it is, she has
to commit infanticide in the winter:

> Farewell, unblessed, unfriended child,
> I cannot bear to watch thee die!

Even so perceptive a reader as Fanny Ratchford only "gradually and very reluctantly"[4] came to the recognition of gratuitous
infanticide on the part of Rosina (or A.G.A. or Geraldine). As
Leicester Bradner has pointed out, Emily Brontë seems to have
been obsessed with the vision of a young, lovely, happy child
growing up to a life of misery and/or crime. Death for the
child would clearly be better than life.[5] Poem after poem expresses the sense of an experience having the force of absolute
possession, known in childhood, and recoverable only in death
—as though infanticide has a kind of religious justification.
Thus death and childhood are firmly linked in Emily Brontë's
chain of associations.

Another link in the chain is the prevalence of pain as an ele-
mentary condition of life. In *Wuthering Heights*, the wild
eruptions of cruelty and violence are so vivid that one tends not
to notice how frequently pain is inflicted just as a matter of
course. Pinching, slapping, and hair pulling occur constantly.
Catherine wakes Nelly Dean up, not by shaking her gently, but
by pulling her hair. Nelly Dean hears a "manual check" given

---

[4] Fanny Ratchford, *Gondal's Queen* (Austin, Texas, 1955), p. 122*n*.
[5] Leicester Bradner, "The Growth of *Wuthering Heights*," PMLA, XLVIII (1933),
129–146.

to Cathy's saucy mouth. When Catherine first dined at the Lintons', she was "as merry as she could be, dividing her food between the little dog and Skulker, whose nose she pinched as he ate; and kindling a spark of spirit in the vacant blue eyes of the Lintons." Later she is so joyous that "should the meanest thing alive slap me on the cheek, I'd not only turn the other, but, I'd ask pardon for provoking it."

Pain, inflicted by cutting or stabbing, forms the crux of numerous metaphors. Nelly Dean speaks of a "frosty air that cut about her shoulders as keen as a knife." On one occasion, Isabella shrieked "as if witches were running red-hot needles into her." When Hareton timidly put out a hand to stroke one of Cathy's curls, "he might have struck a knife into her neck, she started round in such a taking." Linton "averred that the stab of a knife could not inflict a worse pang than he suffered at seeing his lady vexed."

In like manner, pain is frequently suggested by threats of choking, throttling, suffocating, or strangling. Thus Linton Heathcliff, always on the verge of "choking," does not want Cathy to kiss him because he is afraid of losing his breath. Heathcliff threatens to "strangle" Cathy if she won't be quiet. Even adjectives and verbs suggest choking. The falling snow is "suffocating." Hareton "smothered the storm in a brutal curse." Visitors are "smothered in cloaks and furs."[6]

In summary, then, the world of *Wuthering Heights* is a world of sadism, violence, and wanton cruelty, wherein the children—without the protection of their mothers—have to fight for very life against adults who show almost no tenderness, love, or mercy. Normal emotions are almost completely

---

[6] Mark Schorer notes that "Emily Brontë roots her analogies in the fierce life of animals and in the relentless life of the elements—fire, wind, water." "Fiction and the 'Matrix of Analogy,'" *Kenyon Review*, XI (1949), 545. In addition many of her most effective analogies are rooted in pain—cutting, stabbing, and choking.

inverted: hate replaces love, cruelty replaces kindness, and survival depends on one's ability to be tough, brutal, and rebellious.

II

When one considers the almost unbearable danger of pain
and death to which children are subject in *Wuthering Heights*,
one is struck by the terrible irony of the fact that, after her
death, Catherine wishes to return—and indeed does return—
not as an adult, but as a child. Nelly Dean was overly senti-
mental, but factually correct, in describing her death to Heathcliff: "She lies with a sweet smile on her face; and her latest
ideas wandered back to pleasant early days." How terrible
those early days were is only too apparent; yet her desire to
return to them becomes clear if we understand her character
fully.

As a child Catherine is endowed with a kind of masculine
power that only the most hardened adults usually possess; she
has most unchild-like resources for self-control, endurance, and
sustained rebellion; and she can easily cope with pain. Her
choice of toy is a whip. Nelly Dean remembers her as a wild,
vicious little thing: "She had ways with her such as I never saw
a child take up before; and she put all of us past our patience
fifty times and oftener in a day." "She was never so happy as
when we were all scolding her at once, and she defying us with
her bold, saucy look, and her ready words." So tough was she
that she could actually laugh at punishment. Her greatest
pleasure was to run away with Heathcliff to the moors in the
morning and remain there all day. The after punishment could
be assuaged by simply contriving "some naughty plan of revenge." By the time she visits Thrushcross Grange, she is able
to shrug off pain with amazing ease. Heathcliff reports: "We
ran from the top of the Heights to the park, without stopping—

Catherine completely beaten in the race; because she was bare-foot." During the same experience, she is bitten by a bull-dog, and though "sick . . . from pain," she calls out to Heathcliff, not to save her, but to save himself. "She did not yell out—no! She would have scorned to do it, if she had been spitted on the horns of a mad cow."

During this early period (the Thrushcross Grange episode obviously marks her entrance into puberty—she is twelve years old, has just lost one father whom she could easily manage, and acquired a substitute whom she could not), she never cries, or loses confidence in herself, and never relaxes her arrogant poise.

At the same time Heathcliff proves to be so self-possessed that he too is beyond intimidation by pain or suffering. When Hindley fells him with an iron weight over the argument about colts, Nelly Dean is surprised "to witness how coolly the child gathered himself up, and went on with his intention; exchanging saddles and all, and then sitting down on a bundle of hay to overcome the qualm which the violent blow occasioned, before he entered the house."

Together these almost monstrous "children" establish a mystic bond, forged in pain, and expressed in rebellion. They feel an absolute identification with each other. Heathcliff cannot imagine himself and Catherine behaving like Edgar Linton and Isabella: "When would you catch me wishing to have what Catherine wanted? to find us by ourselves, seeing entertainment in yelling, and sobbing, and rolling on the ground, divided by the whole room?" And Catherine is just as dedicated. "I am Heathcliff," she insists—and so long as she can fully identify with him, she is strong.

The intensity of their bond is frequently conveyed in suggestions of incest and child sexuality. Heathcliff may easily be Catherine's half-brother—at least we are invited to entertain that suspicion[7]—and Catherine almost always uses the imagery of incest to express her love for Heathcliff: "the same daemonic substance." She and Heathcliff sleep together until she is over twelve years old, and she cries for the first time when Hindley separates them as bed partners.

The disintegration of Catherine's personality begins with the Thrushcross Grange episode. She fails to see that her entrance into puberty requires a radical change in her relation with Heathcliff, and cannot understand his behaviour after her return to Wuthering Heights. Her attitude towards him remains as it was before puberty, but he recoils "with angry suspicion from her girlish caresses." In his presence she exhibits the same masculine endurance of pain and contempt for weakness that had characterized her childhood. When Heathcliff dashes hot apple sauce in Edgar Linton's face, she blames Edgar for provoking him, adding, "he'll be flogged; I hate him to be flogged! I can't eat my dinner," and she scorns Edgar's sobbing with the contemptuous remark, "well, don't cry . . . you're not killed." She herself cries, in sympathy for Heathcliff, but only after a valiant effort to hold back the tears.

Even after her marriage, she is tough and masculine in the presence of Heathcliff. She condemns her husband for crying, scorns his "whining for trifles" and "idle petulance." She takes Heathcliff's side in his climactic fight with Edgar, and her pitilessness is truly awesome. "If you have not courage to attack him," she says to her husband, "make an apology, or allow yourself to be beaten."

---

[7] Mr. Earnshaw never quite explains why he brought Heathcliff to Wuthering Heights in the first place, nor—and more suspiciously—why he prefers Heathcliff to his other children. "Where did he come from, the little dark thing, harboured by a good man to his bane?" asks Nelly Dean of herself, quite gratuitously, as though to prompt the reader. Eric Solomon has recently noted the "vague incestuous aura over the entire plot of *Wuthering Heights*," and adds that if Catherine and Heathcliff are really sister and brother "the tragedy of *Wuthering Heights* is increased in intensity and inevitability." "The Incest Theme in *Wuthering Heights*," NCF, XIV (1959), 80–83.

The source of her strength, however, is Heathcliff. Without him, she gradually finds herself unable to endure pain or to keep her self-possession, and her temper becomes uncontrollable. During Edgar Linton's last visit to Wuthering Heights, she loses her poise in a dispute with Heathcliff, after which she pinches and slaps Nelly Dean, lies about it, shakes little Hareton "till the poor child waxed livid," boxes Edgar on the ear, insists "I did nothing deliberately," and begins weeping "in serious earnest." As she grows older, pain becomes intolerable; she cries on the slightest provocation and resorts easily to fits of petulance and self-pity. "Our fiery Catherine was no better than a wailing child," remarks Nelly Dean of the grown woman who could "beat Hareton, or any child, at a good passionate fit of crying."

Her marriage to Linton serves only to weaken her, and the open break between Heathcliff and Linton finally destroys her completely. She resorts to "senseless, wicked rages." "There she lay dashing her head against the arm of the sofa, and grinding her teeth, so that you might fancy she would crash them to splinters." The girl who could once hold off a whole household of angry adults now loses all self-possession. She imagines that everyone is against her: "I thought, though everybody hated and despised each other, they could not avoid loving me. And they have all turned to enemies in a few hours: *they* have, I'm positive; the people *here*." Her fantasies are almost as terrifying as her dreams, and her dreams "appal" her. By this time she has completely lost her grip on reality. She sees a face in the black press which isn't there. "Oh! Nelly, the room is haunted! I'm afraid of being alone!"

In the brief life of Catherine, then, there is a complete reversal of roles. As a child she is an adult; even her sauciness is grounded in inner strength. As an adult she becomes a child, and the pain of living proves intolerable. "I wish I were a girl again," she cries pathetically, "half savage and hardy, and free; and laughing at injuries, not maddening under them." She remembers that she was once strong and knows she is strong no longer. Logically enough, therefore, in her ghostly state, she assumes the role, not of a lovely lady in the lonely moors calling for her lover (which would surely be the "romantic" expectation), but of a little girl come back "home."[8]

III

While Catherine's return in the role of a child fulfils her yearning to regain her childhood strength, it also betrays the fact that only as a child was she ever able to love Heathcliff. After puberty, she is never able to transform her childish passion for identity ("I am Heathcliff," she says—but one does not mate with one's self, with one's kind) into a passion for the union of opposites. Her marriage to Linton, a weak, respectable, undemanding person, is essentially an escape from the demands of adult sexuality, and she sees no betrayal of Heathcliff in the escape. To her, Heathcliff is, and always will be, her wild "childhood" lover; Linton is her respectable "adult" lover, and the two are perfectly compatible. She is never jealous of Heathcliff and cannot understand his jealousy of her; she simply thinks of her "love" for him as entirely different from her "love" for Linton.

Indeed she is correct. The "love" she can offer Heathcliff is precisely the love she offered him as a child—tough, masculine "identity," born in pain, expressed in pain—but nothing like normal adult love: no eroticism, no sex, no pleasure, no satis-

---

[8] On the subject of Emily Brontë's passion for home, J. C. Smith writes "The love of home is her ruling passion, of the home of her childhood." "Emily Brontë: A Reconsideration," *Essays and Studies*, V (1914), 144. Richard Chase contends "childhood is in fact the central theme of Emily Brontë's writing." "The Brontës: A Centennial Observance," *Kenyon Review*, IX (1947), 505.

faction.[9] *Her* "love" is expressed through pain, hate, and relentless recrimination. Hair-pulling and pinching are her modes of physical expression. Surely no more sexless and abnormal scene can be imagined than the final love scene between herself and Heathcliff:[10] "I shouldn't care what you suffered. I care nothing for your sufferings. Why shouldn't *you* suffer?" she says to him. And he can only respond in kind: "Is it not sufficient for your infernal selfishness, that while you are at peace I shall writhe in the torments of hell?" They can meet only in pain and distress: "should a word of mine distress you hereafter, think I feel the same distress underground."

Because Catherine had been unable to meet the demands of adult sexuality, Heathcliff takes revenge by imposing adult sexuality on children, her child and his. The "love" between Linton and Cathy is the ghastly obverse of the love between their parents. Whereas the parents were passionately devoted to each other but could find no fulfilling means of expression, the young ones have the means of expression forced upon them even though they find each other totally repulsive. Linton cannot endure women. At one point having been tortured enough with Cathy's presence, he is granted permission—to his unspeakable relief—to sleep with Hareton. Eventually, however, Linton is killed. The revenge is complete.[11]

---

[9] The abnormality of their love is reflected in Emily Brontë's numerous love poems, about which Charles Morgan notes that "no love poems have ever been more free than hers of erotic imagery." "Emily Brontë," *The Great Victorians*, ed. H. J. and Hugh Massingham (New York, 1932), p. 76.

[10] One suspects some critics of reading this scene with tears in their eyes. Thus James Fotheringham has it that "Heathcliff pours out his whole passion, edged with irony and a sense of wrong,—Catherine faded, spent, but beautiful, fascinating as ever—Heathcliff struggling between a passionate love and a passionate revolt, cruel and tender in one molten mood of hopeless love." "The work of Emily Brontë and the Brontë Problem," *Transactions of the Brontë Society*, II (1900), 122. This is ridiculous: Heathcliff does not indulge (here) in irony; his sense of wrong is certainly not "edged"; Catherine can scarcely be as "beautiful" as ever; Heathcliff is not "tender," and his mood is neither "molten" nor "hopeless."

[11] Despite the obvious isolation of the Wuthering Heights area from the rest of

IV

With the killing of Linton, the terrible implications of the infanticide theme become clear : since childhood is the source of perversity, children are quite logically feared, hated, and finally killed. It was the "child" in Catherine that destroyed the love between her and Heathcliff; it is the "child" in Linton that Heathcliff hates : he imposes adult "love" on his son and Cathy with the full knowledge that such love is absolutely unendurable. An eye for an eye, a tooth for a tooth.[12]

The great love story of *Wuthering Heights*, then, begins in perversity and ends in perversity.[13] The "love" between Catherine and Heathcliff grows under the terrible threat of infanticide, never undergoes a metamorphosis into maturity, and so culminates in revenge on the next generation. The only escape is death; and both Catherine and Heathcliff deeply yearn to die. "The thing that irks me most is this shattered prison, after all," says Catherine. "I'm tired of being enclosed here. I'm wearying

England, some critics insist on seeing social significance in the "rebellion of Heathcliff." Thus Arnold Kettle identifies Heathcliff with the working class, "physically and spiritually degraded by the conditions and relationships of this same [Victorian] society." "Emily Brontë," *An Introduction to the English Novel* (London, 1951), I, 154. This seems to me to limit (and to distort) the meaning of Heathcliff's rebellion. Mr. Kettle correctly reminds us that "Heathcliff was not born in the pages of Byron, but in a Liverpool slum" (p. 139). The more important facts are that Heathcliff was born a gypsy and that he very often acts and talks as though he had just put down a volume of Byron.

[12] In my opinion, Heathcliff as an artistic creation is thoroughly unconvincing. The most effective indictments of Heathcliff have been by Muriel Spark and Derek Stanford, *Emily Brontë* (London, 1953), pp. 254–256; and by Mary Visick, *The Genesis of Wuthering Heights* (Hong Kong, 1958), pp. 74–81. The most effective champion of Heathcliff remains May Sinclair, *The Three Brontës* (Boston and New York, 1912), pp. 244–252.

[13] Lord David Cecil says that "Emily Brontë's vision of life does away with the ordinary antithesis between good and evil." "Emily Brontë and *Wuthering Heights*," *Early Victorian Novelists* (London, 1934), p. 154. C. Day Lewis insists that in the novel's "lurid and uncompromising antinomianism . . . passion is substituted for grace as the justification for an over-riding of the moral law." *Notable Images of Virtue* (Toronto, 1954), p. 10. See also Ruth M. Adams, "*Wuthering Heights*: The Land East of Eden," *NCF*, XIII (1958), 59.

to escape into that glorious world, and to be always there . . .
really with it, and in it." And Heathcliff is just as eager for
death. As soon as he has killed his son, he deliberately wills his
own death. These people take the measure of life and choose to
die, simply because life offers no fulfilment. In the end, the
shepherd boy sees "Heathcliff and a woman" (no longer a
child) now roaming freely and happily about the moors. But
such a consummation could never come in life. Life is pain,
hate, and perversity. It is a tribute to Emily Brontë's uncanny
poetic powers that she has deceived generations of readers into
believing that they were reading a beautiful, romantic, and
indeed glorious love story.[14]

---

[14] The intention of this analysis has been, at least partly, to invalidate such interpretations as represented by Melvin R. Watson: "*Wuthering Heights*, then, is a
psychological study of an elemental man whose soul is torn between love and hate
. . . In Heathcliff one looks in vain for Christian morals or virtues; his is a primitive,
pagan soul; yet love conquers even a Heathcliff in the end." "Tempest in the Soul:
The Theme and Structure of *Wuthering Heights*," NCF, IV (1949), 89–90. This interpretation seems to me to concede far too much to the power of love (in the sense of
"Christian morals or virtues"). It implies a purging of evil in Heathcliff's soul. Love
conquers hate. To my mind this is nonsense. Heathcliff feels no tug between "love"
and "hate"; he makes no concessions to love or to traditional morality; in the end he
simply becomes exhausted. When love does conquer hate—as in the love of young
Cathy for Hareton—Victorian respectability triumphs in the form of symbolic emascu-
lation; Cathy polishes and teaches all the roughness out of Hareton. On this point see
Dorothy Van Ghent, "The Window Figure and the Two-Children Figure in *Wuthering Heights*," NCF, VII (1952), 189–197. But such a triumph is gained at a terrible
cost. As Mark Schorer has it: "Moral magnificence? Not at all; rather, a devastating
spectacle of human waste; ashes." "Technique as Discovery," in *Forms of Modern
Fiction*, ed. William Van O'Connor (Minneapolis, 1948), p. 14. The same point is
made by G. D. Klingopulos, "The Novel as Dramatic Poem (II): *Wuthering Heights*,"
Scrutiny, XIV (1947), 284.

The Implacable, Belligerent People of "Wuthering Heights" *

V. S. PRITCHETT

I HAVE BEEN reading *Wuthering Heights* again, after twenty years, a novel which is often regarded as poetical, mystical and fabulous. No people like Heathcliff and Catherine, it is said, ever existed. *Wuthering Heights* is indeed a poetical novel; but when I was reading it, it seemed to me the most realistic statement about the Yorkshire people of the isolated moorland and dales that I have ever read. I am a southerner; but I spent a good deal of my childhood in those Northern cottages and I recognize the implacable, belligerent people of Emily Brontë's novel at once. The trap used to pick you up at the branch line station and in a few miles you were on the moors, the wind standing against you like an enemy, the moorland drizzle making wraiths over the endless scene, and the birds whimpering in cries of farewell, like parting ghosts. Austere, empty, ominous were the earth and sky, and the air was fiercer and more violent than in the South. The occasional small stone houses stuck up like forts, the people themselves seemed, to a south-

* An extract from "Books in General" which appeared in *The New Statesman and Nation*, 22nd June 1946, and now reprinted by permission of the *New Statesman*.

erner, as stern as soldiers, and even the common sentences they spoke were so turned that, but for a quizzical glitter in the eyes of the speaker, one might have taken their words as challenge, insult or derision. I do not mean that these remote Yorkshire people were not kindly and hospitable folk; but one had not to live among them for long, before one found that their egotism was naked, their hatred unending. They seemed to revel in an hostility which they called frankness or bluntness; but which—how can I put it?—was an attempt to plant all they were, all they could be, all they represented as people, unyielding before you. They expected you to do the same. They despised you if you did not. They had the combative pride of clansmen and, on their lonely farms, clans they were and had been for hundreds of years. I can think of episodes in my own childhood among them which are as extraordinary as some of the things in *Wuthering Heights*; and which, at first sight, would strike the reader as examples of pitiable hatred and harshness. Often they were. But really their fierceness in criticism, the pride, and the violence of their sense of sin was the expression of a view of life which put energy and the will of man above everything else. To survive in these parts, one had to dominate and oppose.

There is no other novel in the English language like *Wuthering Heights*. It is unique first of all for its lack of psychological dismay. Never, in a novel, did so many people hate each other with such zest, such Northern zest. There is a faint, homely pretence that Nelly, the housekeeper and narrator, is a kindly, garrulous old body; but look at her. It is not concealed that she is a spy, a go-between, a secret opener of letters. She is a wonderful character, as clear and round as any old nurse in Richardson or Scott; but no conventional sentiment encases her. She is as hard as iron and takes up her station automatically in the battle. Everyone hates, no one disguises evil in this book; no one is "nice." How refreshing it is to come across a Victorian novel

L

which does not moralize, and yet is very far from amoral. How strange, in Victorian fiction, to see passion treated as the natural pattern of life. How refreshing to see the open skirmishing of egotism, and to see life crackling like a fire through human beings; a book which *feels* human beings, as they feel to themselves. . . .

. . . The power of *Wuthering Heights* grows and is sustained by its plain language and because, at no point, does the writer forget the detail of house or moorland. The storm is intolerable because we have to stand resisting it with our feet clinging to the earth; Emily Brontë would be lost if that storm became rhetorical. But I am one of those who are not carried on by the second part of the story. I can see its moral necessity, but I do not *feel* its logic. Grotesque elements bob up at the break between the two tales. To hear afterwards that Catherine was in advanced pregnancy during the wonderful last scene with Heathcliff, which seems to me the highest moment in the English literature of passionate love, is a physical offence. And then in the beating-up scene later, when Heathcliff breaks in and starts his Dachau act, there are descriptive excesses. One grins back at his "cannibal face" with its "sharp teeth" at the window; and when, on top of all this, Hareton comes in and announces he has been hanging puppies, one lets out the laugh one had reserved for the murder of the children in *Jude the Obscure*. This is just Gothic stuff. The second Catherine has her captivation, but you feel she is a poor creature to fall for Hareton whose long history as a problem-child will take a lot of living down. We have entered the field of psychological realism and social allegory and we are not sure that we have the proper guide. I do not mean that this part of the book is less well written. The characters, the incident, the scene are just as well done as in the earlier part, which is to say that they are beautifully done; and there is always the irresistible pleasure of seeing the wheel turn full circle. But the high power has gone, the storm has spent its force, Heathcliff has become a set character; the devil—and this is surely a decline—has become vicious instead of diabolical. Only, in the last pages, when he fancies he sees the first Catherine again and when, starving himself to death, he begins to relive that ineluctable love, does the power return. And those last pages reconcile us to the moral necessity of the second part of a novel which is not, as some have said, carelessly constructed, but unevenly felt.

On "Wuthering Heights"*

DOROTHY VAN GHENT

EMILY BRONTË's single novel is, of all English novels, the most treacherous for the analytical understanding to approach. It is treacherous not because of failure in its own formal controls on its meaning—for the book is highly wrought in form—but because it works at a level of experience that is unsympathetic to, or rather, simply irrelevant to the social and moral reason. One critic has spoken of the quality of feeling in this book as "a quality of suffering":

> It has anonymity. It is not complete. Perhaps some ballads represent it in English, but it seldom appears in the main stream, and few writers are in touch with it. It is a quality of experience the expression of which is at once an act of despair and an act of recognition or of worship. It is the recognition of an absolute hierarchy. This is also the feeling in Aeschylus. It is found amongst genuine peasants and is a great strength. Developing in places which yield only the permanent essentials of existence, it is undistracted and universal.[1]

We feel the lack of "completeness," which this critic refers to, in the nature of the dramatic figures that Emily Brontë uses; they are figures that arise on and enact their drama on some

---

[1] G. D. Klingopulos, "The Novel as Dramatic Poem (II): *Wuthering Heights*," in *Scrutiny*, XIV: 4 (1946–1947).

ground of the psychic life where ethical ideas are not at home, at least such ethical ideas as those that inform our ordinary experience of the manners of men. They have the "anonymity" of figures in dreams or in religious ritual. The attitude towards life that they suggest is rather one of awed contemplation of an unregenerate universe than a feeling for values or disvalues in types of human intercourse. It is an attitude that is expressed in some of the great Chinese paintings of the Middle Ages, where the fall of a torrent from an enormous height, or a single huge wave breaking under the moon, or a barely indicated chain of distant mountains lost among mists, seems to be animated by some mysterious, universal, half-divine life which can only be "recognized," not understood.

The strangeness that sets *Wuthering Heights* apart from other English novels does not lie alone in the attitude that it expresses and the level of experience that it defines, for something of the same quality of feeling exists, for instance, in Conrad's work. Its strangeness is the perfect simplicity with which it presents its elemental figures almost naked of the web of civilized habits, ways of thinking, forms of intercourse, that provides the familiar background of other fiction. Even Conrad's adventurers, no matter how far they may go into the "heart of darkness," carry with them enough threads of this web to orient them socially and morally. We can illustrate what we mean by this simplicity, this almost nakedness, if we compare Emily Brontë's handling of her materials with Richardson's handling of materials that, in some respects, are similar in kind. For example, the daemonic character of Heathcliff, associated as it is with the wildness of heath and moors, has a recognizable kinship with that of Lovelace, daemonic also, though associated with town life and sophisticated manners. Both are, essentially, an anthropomorphized primitive energy, concentrated in activity, terrible in effect. But Emily Brontë

insists on Heathcliff's gypsy lack of origins, his lack of orientation and determination in the social world, his equivocal status
on the edge of the human. When Mr. Earnshaw first brings the
child home, the child is an "it," not a "he," and "dark almost
as if it came from the devil," and one of Nelly Dean's last re-
flections is, "Is he a ghoul or a vampire?" But Richardson's
Lovelace has all sorts of social relationships and determinations,
an ample family, economic orientation, college acquaintances, a
position in a clique of young rakes; and Richardson is careful,
through Lovelace's own pen, to offer various rationalizations of
his behaviour, each in some degree cogent. So with the whole
multifold *Clarissa*-myth: on all sides it is supported for the
understanding by historically familiar morality and manners.
But *Wuthering Heights* is almost bare of such supports in social
rationalization. Heathcliff might *really* be a demon. The passion of Catherine and Heathcliff is too simple and undeviating
in its intensity, too uncomplex, for us to find in it any echo of
practical social reality. To say that the motivation of this passion
is "simple" is not to say that it is easy to define: much easier to
define are the motivations that are somewhat complex and
devious, for this is the familiar nature of human motivations.
We might associate perfectly "simple" motivations with animal
nature or extra-human nature, but by the same token the quality
of feeling involved would resist analysis.

But this nakedness from the web of familiar morality and
manners is not quite complete. There is the framework by the
convention of narration (the "point of view"): we see the drama
through the eyes of Lockwood and Nelly Dean, who belong
firmly to the world of practical reality. Sifted through the idiom
of their commonplace vision, the drama taking place among the
major characters finds contact with the temporal and the secular. Because Lockwood and Nelly Dean have witnessed the
incredible violence of the life at the Heights, or rather, because

Nelly Dean has witnessed the full span and capacity of that violence and because Lockwood credits her witness, the drama is oriented in the context of the psychologically familiar. There is also another technical bulwark that supports this uneasy tale in the social and moral imagination, and that is its extension over the lives of two generations and into a time of ameliorated and respectable manners. At the end, we see young Cathy teaching Hareton his letters and correcting his boorishess (which, after all, is only the natural boorishness consequent on neglect, and has none of the cannibal unregeneracy of Heathcliff in it); the prospect is one of decent, socially responsible domesticity. For this part of the tale, Lockwood alone is sufficient witness; and the fact that now Nelly Dean's experienced old eyes and memory can be dispensed with assures us of the present reasonableness and objectivity of events, and even infects retrospection on what has happened earlier—making it possible for the dream-rejecting reason to settle complacently for the "naturalness" of the entire story. If ghosts have been mentioned, if the country people swear that Heathcliff "walks," we can, with Lockwood at the end, affirm our scepticism as to "how anyone could ever imagine unquiet slumbers for the sleepers in that quiet earth."

Let us try to diagram these technical aspects of the work, for the compositional soundness of *Wuthering Heights* is owing to them. We may divide the action of the book into two parts, following each other chronologically, the one associated with the earlier generation (Hindley and Catherine and Heathcliff, Edgar and Isabella Linton), the other with the later generation (young Cathy and Linton and Hareton). The first of these actions is centred in what we shall call a "mythological romance"—for the astonishingly ravenous and possessive, perfectly amoral love of Catherine and Heathcliff belongs to that realm of the imagination where myths are created. The second action, centred in the protracted effects of Heathcliff's revenge, involves two sets of young lives and two small "romances": the childish romance of Cathy and Linton, which Heathcliff manages to pervert utterly; and the successful assertion of a healthy, culturally viable kind of love between Cathy and Hareton, asserted as Heathcliff's cruel energies flag and decay. Binding the two "actions" is the perduring figure of Heathcliff himself, demon-lover in the first, paternal ogre in the second. Binding them also is the framing narrational convention or "point of view": the voices of Nelly Dean and Lockwood are always in our ears; one or the other of them is always present at a scene, or is the confidant of someone who was present; through Lockwood we encounter Heathcliff at the beginning of the book, and through his eyes we look on Heathcliff's grave at the end. Still another pattern that binds the two actions is the repetition of what we shall call the "two children" figure—two children raised virtually as brother and sister, in a vibrant relationship of charity and passion and real or possible metamorphosis. The figure is repeated, with variation, three times, in the relationships of the main characters. Of this we shall speak again later. The technical continuities or patterning of the book could, then, be simplified in this way:

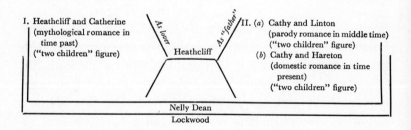

What, concretely, is the effect of this strict patterning and binding? What does it "mean"? The design of the book is drawn in the spirit of intense compositional rigour, of *limitation*; the characters act in the spirit of passionate immoderacy, of *excess*. Let us consider this contrast a little more closely. Essentially, *Wuthering Heights* exists for the mind as a tension between two kinds of reality: the raw, inhuman reality of anonymous natural energies, and the restrictive reality of civilized habits, manners, and codes. The first kind of reality is given to the imagination in the violent figures of Catherine and Heathcliff, portions of the flux of nature, children of rock and heath and tempest, striving to identify themselves as human, but disrupting all around them with their monstrous appetite for an inhuman kind of intercourse, and finally disintegrated from within by the very energies out of which they are made. It is this vision of a reality radically alien from the human that the ancient Chinese landscape paintings offer also. But in those ancient paintings there is often a tiny human figure, a figure that is obviously that of a philosopher, for instance, or that of a peasant—in other words, a human figure decisively belonging to and representing a culture—who is placed in diminutive perspective beside the enormously cascading torrent, or who is seen driving his water buffalo through the overwhelming mists or faceless snows; and this figure is outlined sharply, so that, though it is extremely tiny, it is very definite in the giant surrounding indefiniteness. The effect is one of contrast between finite and infinite, between the limitation of the known and human, and the unlimitedness of the unknown and the non-human. So also in *Wuthering Heights*: set over against the wilderness of inhuman reality is the quietly secular, voluntarily limited, safely human reality that we find in the gossipy concourse of Nelly Dean and Lockwood, the one an old family servant with a strong grip on the necessary emotional economies that make life endurable, the other a city visitor in the country, a man whose very disinterestedness and facility of feeling and

attention indicate the manifold emotional economies by which
city people particularly protect themselves from any disturbing
note of the ironic discord between civilized life and the insen-
tient wild flux of nature in which it is islanded. This second
kind of reality is given also in the romance of Cathy and Hareton, where book learning and gentled manners and domestic
charities form a little island of complacence. The tension between these two kinds of reality, their inveterate opposition and
at the same time their *continuity* one with another, provides at
once the content and the form of *Wuthering Heights*. We see
the tension graphically in the diagram given above. The inhuman excess of Heathcliff's and Catherine's passion, an excess
that is carried over into the second half of the book by Heathcliff's revenge, an excess everywhere present in language[2]—in
verbs and modifiers and metaphors that seethe with a brute fury
—this excess is held within a most rigorous pattern of repeated
motifs and of what someone has called the "Chinese box" of
Nelly Dean's and Lockwood's interlocution. The form of the
book, then—a form that may be expressed as a tension between
the impulse to excess and the impulse to limitation or economy
—*is* the content. The form, in short, is the book itself. Only in
the fully wrought, fully realized, work of art does form so
exhaust the possibilities of the material that it identifies itself
with these possibilities.

If there has been any cogency in what we have said above, we
should ask now how it is that the book is able to represent
dramatically, in terms of human "character," its vision of the
inhuman. After all, Catherine and Heathcliff *are* "characters,"
and not merely molecular vibrations in the primordial surge of
things; indeed, they are so credibly characterized that Holly-

---

[2] Mark Schorer examines this aspect of *Wuthering Heights* in his essay "Fiction and
the 'Analogical Matrix,'" in *Critiques and Essays on Modern Fiction* (New York: The
Ronald Press Company, 1952).

wood has been able to costume and cosmeticize them. As "characters," what are they? As lovers, what kind of love is theirs? They gnash and foam at each other. One could borrow for them a line from a poem by John Crowe Ransom describing lovers in hell: "Stuprate, they rend each other when they kiss." This is not "romantic love," as that term has popular meaning; and it is not even sexual love, naturalistically considered—the impulse to destruction is too pure in it, too simple and direct. Catherine says she *is* Heathcliff, and the implication is not of the possibility of a "mating," for one does not "mate" with oneself. Similarly, after her death, when Heathcliff howls that he cannot live without his *life*, he cannot live without his *soul* (and Nellie says that he "howled, not like a man, but like a savage beast"), the relationship and the destiny suggested are not those of adult human lovers, because the complex attendant motivations of adult life are lacking. But the emotional implications of Catherine's and Heathcliff's passion are never "adult," in the sense of there being in that passion any recognition of the domestic and social responsibilities, and the spiritual complexities, of adult life. Whatever could happen to these two, if they could be happily together, would be something altogether asocial, amoral, savagely irresponsible, wildly impulsive: it would be the enthusiastic, experimental, quite random activity of childhood, occult to the socialized adult. But since no conceivable *human* male and female, not brutish, not anthropologically rudimentary, could be together in this way as adults, all that we can really imagine for the grown-up Catherine and Heathcliff, as "characters" on the human plane, is what the book gives of them—their mutual destruction by tooth and nail in an effort, through death, to get back to the lost state of gypsy freedom in childhood.

Caught in the economical forms of adult life—concepts of social and intellectual "betterment" (such as lead Catherine to

marry Edgar Linton), the frames of wealth and property ownership (which Heathcliff at first exploits in order to "raise" himself to Catherine's standard, and then as an engine of revenge
against both the Earnshaws and the Lintons), marital relationships and parenthood—they are, for the imagination, "human-
ized," endowed with "character," at least to the extent that we
see their explosive confusions, resistances, and misery convulsing
the forms usual to human adulthood. Their obsession, their
prime passion, is also "human" although it is utterly destructive
of the values signified by that word : the passion to lose the self
in some "otherness," whether in complete identification with
another person (an identification for which "mating" is a sur-
rogate only of a temporary and lapsing kind), or by absorption
into "nature"—but it is a passion that is tabooed for the socialized adult, disguised, held in check by the complex cultural
economies, safely stabled in the unconscious, at best put to work
in that darkness to turn the mill of other objectives. This re-
gressive passion is seen in uncompromised purity in Catherine
and Heathcliff, and it opens the prospect of disintegration—
disintegration into the unconsciousness of childhood and the
molecular fluidity of death—in a word, into anonymous natural
energy.

If the story of Catherine and Heathcliff had not been a story
told by an old woman as something that had had its inception
many years ago, if the old woman who tells the story had not
been limited in imagination and provincial in her sympathies,
if the story had been dramatized immediately in the here-and-
now and not at a temporal remove and through a dispassioned
intermediator, it is doubtful that it would resonate emotionally
for us or carry any conviction—even any "meaning." Because of
the very fact that the impulses it represents are taboo, they can
conveniently be observed only at a remove, as someone else's, as
of the past, and from the judicial point of view of conventional

manners. The "someone else's" and the "long ago" are the mind's saving convention for making a distance with itself such as will allow it perspective. Thus the technical *displacement* of Heathcliff's and Catherine's story into past time and into the memory of an old woman functions in the same way as dream displacements: it both censors and indulges, protects and liberates.

Significantly, our first real contact with the Catherine–Heathcliff drama is established through a dream—Lockwood's dream of the ghost-child at the window. Lockwood is motivated to dream the dream by the most easily convincing circumstance; he has fallen asleep while reading Catherine's diary, and during his sleep a tempest-blown branch is scratching on the windowpane. But why should Lockwood, the well-mannered urbanite, dream *this*?

I pulled its wrist on to the broken pane, and rubbed it to and fro till the blood ran down and soaked the bedclothes . . .

The image is probably the most cruel one in the book. Hareton's hanging puppies, Heathcliff's hanging the springer spaniel, Hindley's forcing a knife between Nelly's teeth or throwing his baby over the staircase, Catherine's leaving the blue print of her nails on Isabella's arm, Heathcliff stamping on Hindley's face—these images and others like them imply savagery or revengefulness or drunkenness or hysteria, but always a motivating set of emotional circumstances. But this is the punctilious Lockwood—whose antecedents and psychology are so insipid that we care little about them—who scrapes the dream-waif's wrist back and forth on broken glass till the blood runs down and soaks the bedclothes. The cruelty of the dream is the gratuitousness of the violence wrought on a child by an emotionally unmotivated vacationer from the city, dreaming in a strange bed. The bed is an old-fashioned closet bed ("a large

oak case . . . it formed a little closet" with a window set in it):
its panelled sides Lockwood has "pulled together" before going
to sleep. The bed is like a coffin (at the end of the book, Heathcliff dies in it, behind its closed panels); it had been Catherine's
bed, and the movable panels themselves suggest the coffin in
which she is laid, whose "panels" Heathcliff bribes the sexton
to remove at one side. Psychologically, Lockwood's dream has
only the most perfunctory determinations, and nothing at all of
result for the dreamer himself, except to put him uncomfortably
out of bed. But poetically the dream has its reasons, compacted
into the image of the daemonic child scratching at the pane,
trying to get from the "outside" "in," and of the dreamer in a
bed like a coffin, released by that deathly privacy to indiscrimin-
ate violence. The coffin-like bed shuts off any interference with
the wild deterioration of the psyche. Had the dream used any
other agent than the effete, almost epicene Lockwood, it would
have lost this symbolic force; for Lockwood, more successfully
than anyone else in the book, has shut out the powers of darkness (the pun in his name is obvious in this context); and his
lack of any dramatically thorough motivation for dreaming the
cruel dream suggests those powers as existing autonomously,
not only in the "outsideness" of external nature, beyond the
physical windowpane, but also within, even in the soul least
prone to passionate excursion.

The windowpane is the medium, treacherously transparent,
separating the "inside" from the "outside," the "human" from
the alien and terrible "other." Immediately after the incident of
the dream, the time of the narrative is displaced into the childhood of Heathcliff and Catherine, and we see the two children
looking through the window of the Lintons' drawing room.

"Both of us were able to look in by standing on the basement, and
clinging to the ledge, and we saw—ah! it was beautiful—a splendid place
carpeted with crimson, and crimson-covered chairs and tables, and a pure

white ceiling bordered by gold, a shower of glass-drops hanging in silver chains from the centre, and shimmering with little soft tapers. Old Mr. and Mrs. Linton were not there; Edgar and his sister had it entirely to themselves. Shouldn't they have been happy? We should have thought ourselves in heaven!"

Here the two unregenerate waifs look *in* from the night on the heavenly vision of the refinements and securities of the most privileged human estate. But Heathcliff rejects the vision: seeing the Linton children blubbering and bored there (*they* cannot get *out*!), he senses the menace of its limitations; while Catherine is fatally tempted. She is taken in by the Lintons, and now it is Heathcliff alone outside looking through the window.

"The curtains were still looped up at one corner, and I resumed my station as a spy; because, if Catherine had wished to return, I intended shattering their great glass panes to a million of fragments, unless they let her out. She sat on the sofa quietly . . . the woman-servant brought a basin of warm water, and washed her feet; and Mr. Linton mixed a tumbler of negus, and Isabella emptied a plateful of cakes into her lap . . . Afterwards, they dried and combed her beautiful hair . . ."

Thus the first snare is laid by which Catherine will be held for a human destiny—her feet washed, cakes and wine for her delectation, her beautiful hair combed (the motifs here are limpid as those of fairy tale, where the changeling in the "otherworld" is held there mysteriously by bathing and by the strange new food he has been given to eat). By her marriage to Edgar Linton, Catherine yields to that destiny; later she resists it tormentedly and finds her way out of it by death. Literally she "catches her death" by throwing open the window.

"Open the window again wide; fasten it open! Quick, why don't you move?" [she says to Nelly].
"Because I won't give you your death of cold," I answered.
"You won't give me a chance of life, you mean," she said . . .

In her delirium, she opens the window, leans out into the winter wind, and calls across the moors to Heathcliff.

"Heathcliff, if I dare you now, will you venture? . . . Find a way then !
. . . You are slow ! . . . you always followed me !"

On the night after her burial, unable to follow her (though he
digs up her grave in order to lie beside her in the coffin from
which the side panels have been removed), he returns to the
Heights *through the window*—for Hindley has barred the door
—to wreak on the living the fury of his frustration. It is years
later that Lockwood arrives at the Heights and spends his uncomfortable night there. Lockwood's outcry in his dream brings
Heathcliff *to the window*, Heathcliff who has been caught
ineluctably in the human to grapple with its interdictions long
after Catherine has broken through them. The treachery of the
window is that Catherine, lost now in the "other," can look
through the transparent membrane that separates her from
humanity, can scratch on the pane, but cannot get "in," while
Heathcliff, though he forces the window open and howls into
the night, cannot get "out." When he dies, Nelly Dean discovers the window swinging open, the window of that old-
fashioned coffin-like bed where Lockwood had had the dream.
Rain has been pouring in during the night, drenching the dead
man. Nelly says,

I hasped the window; I combed his black long hair from his forehead;
I tried to close his eyes : to extinguish, if possible, that frightful, life-like
gaze of exultation before any one else beheld it. They would not shut :
they seemed to sneer at my attempts . . .

Earlier, Heathcliff's eyes have been spoken of as "the clouded
windows of hell" from which a "fiend" looks out. All the other
uses of the "window" that we have spoken of here are not
figurative but perfectly naturalistic uses, though their symbolic
value is inescapable. But the fact that Heathcliff's eyes refuse to
close in death suggests the symbol in a metaphorical form (the
"fiend" has now got "out," leaving the window open), eluci-

dating with simplicity the meaning of the "window" as a separation between the daemonic depths of the soul and the limited and limiting lucidities of consciousness, a separation between the soul's "otherness" and its humanness.

There is still the difficulty of defining, with any precision, the quality of the daemonic that is realized most vividly in the conception of Heathcliff, a difficulty that is mainly due to our tendency always to give the "daemonic" some ethical status—that is, to relate it to an ethical hierarchy. Heathcliff's is an archetypal figure, untraceably ancient in mythological thought—an imaged recognition of that part of nature which is "other" than the human soul (the world of the elements and the animals) and of that part of the soul itself which is "other" than the conscious part. But since Martin Luther's revival of this archetype for modern mythology, it has tended to forget its relationship with the elemental "otherness" of the outer world and to identify itself solely with the dark functions of the soul. As an image of soul work, it is ethically relevant, since everything that the soul does—even unconsciously, even "ignorantly" (as in the case of Oedipus)—offers itself for ethical judgment, whereas the elements and the animals do not. Puritanism perpetuated the figure for the imagination; Milton gave it its greatest aesthetic splendour, in the fallen angel through whom the divine beauty still shone; Richardson introduced it, in the person of Lovelace, to an infatuated middle class; and always the figure was ethically relevant through the conception of "sin" and "guilt." (Let us note here, however, the ambivalence of the figure, an ambivalence that the medieval devil does not have. The medieval devil is a really ugly customer, so ugly that he can even become a comedy figure—as in the medieval moralities. The daemonic archetype of which we are speaking here is deeply serious in quality because of his ambivalence: he is a fertilizing energy and profoundly attractive, and at the same time horribly de-

M

structive to civilized institutionalism. It is because of his ambivalence that, though he is the "enemy," ethically speaking, he
so easily takes on the stature and beauty of a hero, as he does in
the Satan of *Paradise Lost*.) In Byron's *Manfred*, the archetype
underwent a rather confusing sea-change, for Manfred's crime
is, presumably, so frightful that it cannot be mentioned, and
the indefinable nature of the crime blurs the edges of the figure
and cuts down its resonance in the imagination (when we guess
that the crime might be incest, we are disposed to find this a
rather paltry equation for the Byronic incantation of guilt);
nevertheless, the ethical relevancy of the figure remains. Let us
follow it a little further, before returning to Emily Brontë's
Heathcliff. In the later nineteenth century, in the novels of Dos-
toevski, it reappears with an enormous development of psychological subtlety, and also with a great strengthening and clari-
fication of its ethical significance. In the work of André Gide,
it undergoes another sea-change: the archetypal daemonic
figure now becomes the principle of progress, the spirit of free
investigation and creative experience; with this reorientation, it
becomes positively ethical rather than negatively so. In Thomas
Mann's *Doctor Faustus*, it reverts to its earlier and more constant significance, as the type of the instinctive part of the soul,
a great and fertilizing power, but ethically unregenerate and
therefore a great danger to ethical man.

Our interest in sketching some phases of the history of this
archetype has been to show that it has had, in modern mythology, constantly a status in relation to ethical thought. The
exception is Heathcliff. Heathcliff is no more ethically relevant
than is flood or earthquake or whirlwind. It is as impossible to
speak of him in terms of "sin" and "guilt" as it is to speak in
this way of the natural elements or the creatures of the animal
world. In him, the type reverts to a more ancient mythology
and to an earlier symbolism. *Wuthering Heights* so baffles and

confounds the ethical sense because it is not informed with that sense at all: it is profoundly informed with the attitudes of "animism," by which the natural world—that world which is "other" than and "outside of" the consciously individualized human—*appears* to act with an energy similar to the energies of the soul; to be permeated with soul energy but of a mysterious and alien kind that the conscious human soul, bent on securing itself through civilization, cannot identify itself with as to purpose; an energy that can be propitiated, that can at times be canalized into humanly purposeful channels, that *must* be given religious recognition both for its enormous fertility and its enormous potential destructiveness. But Heathcliff does have human shape and human relationships; he is, so to speak, "caught in" the human; two kinds of reality intersect in him— as they do, with a somewhat different balance, in Catherine; as they do, indeed, in the other characters. Each entertains, in some degree, the powers of darkness—from Hindley, with his passion for self-destruction (he, too, wants to get "out"), to Nelly Dean, who in a sense "propitiates" those powers with the casuistry of her actions, and even to Lockwood, with his sadistic dream. Even in the weakest of these souls there is an intimation of the dark Otherness, by which the soul is related psychologically to the inhuman world of pure energy, for it carries within itself an "otherness" of its own, that inhabits below consciousness.

The Style of
"Wuthering Heights"*

IRENE COOPER WILLIS

THE MANUSCRIPT of *Wuthering Heights* has never been found. Nor is there any record of its having been preserved. We do not even know if it was in existence and referred to by Charlotte Brontë in 1850, when she was preparing the second edition of the book after her sisters' deaths. We know that Emily Brontë's own copy of the first edition was in Charlotte's possession, for Mr. Clement Shorter, in his introduction to an edition published in 1911, stated that the text of that edition had been set up from this same copy, which he had obtained from Charlotte's husband, Mr. Nicholls, who died as late as 1906. Apparently, no one knows what became of the manuscript.

Thus we are without an important, yet not conclusive, piece of evidence as to the authorship of *Wuthering Heights*. Doubts having arisen, even if the manuscript were suddenly to be discovered, and to be found to be in Emily Brontë's handwriting, doubts would still exist. It would still be possible to argue that Emily had copied, wholly or partly, from a manuscript written by Branwell. It seems, indeed, that those who believe in Branwell's authorship claim no more than this; they do not appear to dispute that the actual circumstances of the publication of the

* Part I of Irene Cooper Willis, *The Authorship of Wuthering Heights* (1936). Reprinted by kind permission of The Hogarth Press Ltd.

book point to its being the work of Emily Brontë, writing under
the pseudonym of "Ellis Bell."

The loss of the manuscript, therefore, is not of great moment
in the dispute. It may even be looked upon as an advantage, in
that it obliges the disputants to examine evidence far more
decisive of authorship than handwriting can be, namely the
literary construction of the book. By literary construction is
meant not merely syntax, but the whole way in which a writer
deals with his material, impressions, ideas and trains of thought,
and arranges or organizes these so as to carry the reader with
him as an interested listener while he tells his tale. This aspect
of writing has been neglected. One reason for the neglect may
be that disputes as to authorship are rare, and do not, in any
case, stir the reading public, who, naturally, are more interested
in a book itself than in the question of who wrote it. Further,
unlike a picture, enjoyment of which can only be got from the
original painting, a book, through publication, is immediately
reproduced a thousandfold and more, and, consequently, what
gives the original painting its unique value and stimulates a
study of its technique is lacking in the case of literature. Besides,
literature is a very mixed art; the appeal of a book has often
little to do with its purely literary qualities. And, oddly enough
—and this is perhaps the chief reason why literary craftsman-
ship is not generally recognized, let alone studied—the greatest
literature, in the novel form, is that which least of all draws
attention to those literary qualities, seeming, to all appearances,
to have been written intuitively and without any technical forethought. As indeed it probably was written. But though the
writer himself may be unconscious of his art, just as he is unconscious of the way he forms his handwriting, his individual
technique, style, gesture, are there in the structure of his sentences and the grouping of them, in the engineering, so to
speak, of his narrative, and reveal themselves, as unconscious

habits do reveal themselves, as large as the life of the book for those who have eyes to see. "Le style—c'est l'homme." The truth of this famous saying needs to be applied. People have a way of talking about a book as if its author might be anyone who was known to write. *Wuthering Heights* has been claimed as the work of Branwell Brontë on the strength of his much-talked-of conversational brilliancy, his literary ambitions and some hazy statements made by two or three people, years after the events they recalled, to the effect that Branwell had written a great portion, at any rate, of the book. If Branwell's writings, such as they are, showed any likeness to *Wuthering Heights*, there would be reason for treating these statements seriously. But Branwell's writings, other than a few feeble poems quoted by Miss Law, Branwell's chief partisan, do not appear to have been examined to this purpose. Miss Law has, however, studied *Wuthering Heights* and is convinced that "an unmistakable air of masculinity" hangs over every page of it. She says: "The very character of this terrible tale should convince any thoughtful or closely observant reader that no woman's hand ever penned *Wuthering Heights*. Such, indeed, was the universal opinion of the Press when it first appeared."[1]

In passing, it may be observed that it was one specimen of the universal opinion of the Press, referring to the author of *Wuthering Heights* as a "ferocious male," which drew a scornful smile from Emily in her last days, and that a section of the Press had opined that *Wuthering Heights* was written by the author of *Jane Eyre*, over which book Miss Law would probably admit that there hangs "an unmistakable air" of femininity. *Jane Eyre* was also by some people thought to have been written by Thackeray, so that there is evidently a divergence of opinion as to what a man's or a woman's pen can produce. This

---

[1] *Patrick Branwell Brontë*, by Alice Law. A. M. Philpot Ltd.

divergence is in keeping with the recognized psychological view that the mental or psychical make-up of a man or a woman does not always correspond to physical type. Nearly everyone, according to psychological authorities, is a mixture of masculinity and femininity in different proportions.

The discovery of "unmistakable masculinity" in *Wuthering Heights* (whatever its outward and visible signs may be, as to which I do not venture to pronounce) does not therefore carry us very far, certainly not as far as the conclusion that the masculinity proceeded from Branwell. To get anywhere near that conclusion, it is necessary to compare Branwell's productions with *Wuthering Heights* and to see if the same air hangs over the one as over the other.

As the first chapters of *Wuthering Heights* are the ones which Miss Law declares to be most unmistakably masculine, and are also the ones which Mr. Benson, in his *Charlotte Brontë*, is inclined to attribute to Branwell, let us consider the writing of these and examine the following passages.[1]

The first is the passage with which the story opens.

1801—I have just returned from a visit to my landlord—the solitary neighbour that I shall be troubled with. This is certainly a beautiful country! In all England, I do not believe that I could have fixed on a situation so completely removed from the stir of society. A perfect misanthropist's heaven : and Mr. Heathcliff and I are such a suitable pair to divide the desolation between us. A capital fellow! He little imagined how my heart warmed towards him when I beheld his black eyes withdraw so suspiciously under their brows, as I rode up, and when his fingers sheltered themselves with a jealous resolution, still further in his waistcoat, as I announced my name.

"Mr. Heathcliff?" I said.

A nod was the answer.

"Mr. Lockwood, your new tenant, sir. I do myself the honour of calling

---

[1] The extracts from "Wuthering Heights" are taken from the text in The World's Classics (Oxford University Press) 1932 edition, which corresponds with the text of the first edition of the book.

as soon as possible after my arrival, to express the hope that I have not inconvenienced you by my perseverance in soliciting the occupation of Thrushcross Grange : I heard yesterday you had had some thoughts——"

"Thrushcross Grange is my own, sir," he interrupted, wincing. "I should not allow any one to inconvenience me, if I could hinder it—walk in !"

The "walk in" was uttered with closed teeth and expressed the sentiment, "Go to the Deuce" : even the gate over which he leant manifested no sympathizing movement to the words; and I think that circumstances determined me to accept the invitation : I felt interested in a man who seemed more exaggeratedly reserved than myself.

When he saw my horse's breast fairly pushing the barrier, he did pull out his hand to unchain it, and then sullenly preceded me up the causeway, calling, as we entered the court—"Joseph, take Mr. Lockwood's horse; and bring up some wine."

I, personally, can never read this beginning without getting an irritating impression of Lockwood, the diarist of these first scenes and the recipient through Nelly Dean of the long tragic tale. His idea of himself as a hermit is so obviously wrong. Else why should he, immediately after extolling the solitariness of the neighbourhood, rush off to pay a visit to his landlord, four miles away? This irritation increases as the introductory chapters proceed. Reserve is the last thing that Lockwood seems to possess. His second visit to Heathcliff's house, on the day following his first, is nothing short of a forced intrusion. He deserves all the discomfort he endures.

However, putting aside the irritation with Lockwood, accepting him as a mere artifice for introducing the reader to the real story, a lay figure whom the author neglected to make or could not conveniently make other than a contradictory character, this passage is a remarkably alive description of Lockwood's first meeting with Heathcliff. The meeting seems to take place before our very eyes. By attention being drawn to the details of Heathcliff's movements, active watching is set up in our minds, and we get an extra sense of movement by significant features of

Heathcliff being singled out and given an independent activity apart from the rest of his body. "His black eyes withdraw so suspiciously under their brows"—"his fingers shelter themselves with a jealous resolution in his waistcoat." The black eyes and the fingers are, as it were, personified, and this attribution of separate personality to parts of the body which are not separate, supplies a sense of activity corresponding to the activity of the real scene, and makes up to the reader for not actually being there to see what is going on with his own eyes. This device, though to call it such suggests deliberate intention on the author's part which probably was far from being the case, is incessant, from the beginning to the end of *Wuthering Heights*: there is not a page in which it does not occur, and on most pages it occurs several times. Slightly different forms of it are seen in the sentences: "Even *the gate* over which he leant *manifested* no sympathizing movement to the words"—"When he saw my *horse's breast* fairly *pushing* the barrier." Here we have an inanimate object, a gate, and a part of a horse's body endowed with separate activity, and the result is that our attention is fixed, for the moment, just as Lockwood's was, on the particular spot in the scene where movement was taking place.

Writing, as Vernon Lee pointed out in her *Handling of Words*, is an art of substitution of effects. The writer has to find a substitute in words for the movement which in the real scene is going on all the time but which he cannot continually be reiterating. In watching a real scene, the observer is not, of course, aware of how his eye shifts from one point to another; this fact, however, can soon be discovered by experiment. The passage quoted above is one of innumerable examples to be found in *Wuthering Heights* of a very direct method of introducing movement by means of extra accent upon certain focusing words.

In confirmation of this assertion, a much later passage may

be referred to. It occurs in Isabella Linton's story (Chapter XVII), given to Mrs. Dean, after Isabella had fled from Heathcliff. She is describing the scene in the "house" at Wuthering Heights, when Hindley barred the door against his tormentor and threatened to shoot him if he entered. Isabella has just said that secretly she felt that if this threat could be carried out, it would be a blessing. She continues:

> . . . As I sat nursing these reflections, the casement behind me was banged on to the floor by a blow from the latter individual, and his black countenance looked blightingly through. The stanchions stood too close to suffer his shoulders to follow, and I smiled, exulting in my fancied security. His hair and clothes were whitened with snow, and his sharp cannibal teeth, revealed by cold and wrath, gleamed through the dark.

Directness is indeed the outstanding feature of the book. Each sentence goes straight as a dart to the impression sought to be conveyed. Going back to the first chapter, consider this paragraph:

> Wuthering Heights is the name of Mr. Heathcliff's dwelling. "Wuthering" being a significant provincial adjective, descriptive of the atmospheric tumult to which its station is exposed in stormy weather. Pure, bracing ventilation they must have up there at all times, indeed: one may guess the power of the north wind blowing over the edge, by the excessive slant of a few stunted firs at the end of the house; and by a range of gaunt thorns all stretching their limbs one way, as if craving alms of the sun. Happily, the architect had foresight to build it strong: the narrow windows are deeply set in the wall, and the corners defended by large jutting stones.

"*Wuthering Heights is the name of Mr. Heathcliff's dwelling.*" The name, with all that it means to the author and is going to mean to us, comes first. "The name of Mr. Heathcliff's dwelling is Wuthering Heights," a sentence which contains the same information as the other, would not strike the same note. Then comes a parenthesis—" 'Wuthering' being a significant provincial adjective, descriptive of the atmospheric

tumult," etc. Strictly, before this and after "dwelling," there
should be a comma instead of the full stop; nevertheless, the
slip serves to give the remark the appearance of an "aside"
leading up to what follows, when its full force is exposed.
"Pure, bracing ventilation . . . up there, at all times, indeed"
—the writer puts an exclamatory turn into the phrase, besides
introducing a feeling of windiness by the use of the word "ventilation," which is much more suggestive of activity than "air."
It may be only my fancy, but the next sentence seems to me to
give the direction as well as the power of that "north wind
blowing over the edge"; it is an extended sentence and seems in
the actual line of the drive of the gales which wrought that
"excessive slant of a few stunted firs at the end of the house"
and swept onward to that "range of gaunt thorns all stretching
their limbs one way, as if craving alms of the sun." Fancy or
not, however, there is no denying a vivid impression of the way
the wind blows up on those heights, and the assurance, which
the writer hastens to give, as to the strength of the house, is
welcome and restoring to our sense of shaken equilibrium.

Now take the indoors scene and notice how the paint, so to
speak, is put on there.

One step brought us into the family sitting-room, without any introductory lobby or passage : they call it here "the house" pre-eminently. It
includes kitchen and parlour, generally; but I believe at Wuthering
Heights the kitchen is forced to retreat altogether into another quarter :
at least I distinguished a chatter of tongues, and a clatter of culinary
utensils, deep within; and I observed no signs of roasting, boiling, or
baking, about the huge fire-place; nor any glitter of copper saucepans and
tin cullenders on the walls. One end, indeed, reflected splendidly both
light and heat from ranks of immense pewter dishes, interspersed with
silver jugs and tankards, towering row after row, on a vast oak dresser, to
the very roof. The latter had never been underdrawn : its entire anatomy
lay bare to an inquiring eye, except where a frame of wood laden with
oat-cakes and clusters of legs of beef, mutton and ham, concealed it. Above
the chimney were sundry villainous old guns, and a couple of horse-

pistols : and, by way of ornament, three gaudily painted canisters disposed along its ledge. The floor was of smooth, white stone : the chairs, high-backed, primitive structures, painted green : one or two heavy black ones lurking in the shade. In an arch under the dresser, reposed a huge, liver-coloured bitch pointer, surrounded by a swarm of squealing puppies; and other dogs haunted other recesses.

Observe the straightness of the direction of the first sentence —"One step brought us into the family sitting-room"—it marches exactly with the action it describes. Again, see how verbs of movement are used about things which in themselves are motionless, and how, by a change of mood of the verb, from active to passive, variety of movement and also spatial dimension are suggested. "The kitchen is *forced to retreat*"—"one or two heavy black ones [chairs] *lurking* in the shade"—"ranks of immense pewter dishes . . . towering." The roof is given personality; its anatomy is spoken of. Another substantial effect is produced upon the reader by direct emphasis upon Lockwood's visual and audible impressions, "a chatter of tongues"; "a clatter of culinary utensils"; "light and heat from ranks of immense pewter dishes." All this is astonishingly dramatic, yet it does not affect us astonishingly, until we come to examine the structure; in reading it in the ordinary way, we feel merely that we are in close contact with the scene. The technique is as effective as the craft of the stage-furniture maker, who has to cut all decorative detail much more deeply than it would be cut for everyday use, in order that it may be seen at a distance from the front of the stage—where it merely looks like ordinary furniture.

Equally effective is the way in which, in the scene of the disturbance when Lockwood is set upon by the dogs and has to be rescued by the cook, we are made to realize his discomfort and gradual return to composure. I quote the passage in full :

I took a seat at the end of the hearthstone opposite that towards which my landlord advanced, and filled up an interval of silence by attempting to caress the canine mother, who had left her nursery, and was sneaking wolfishly to the back of my legs, her lip curled up, and her white teeth watering for a snatch. My caress provoked a long, guttural gnarl.

"You'd better let the dog alone," growled Mr. Heathcliff in unison, checking fiercer demonstrations with a punch of his foot. "She's not accustomed to be spoiled—not kept for a pet." Then, striding to a side door, he shouted again, "Joseph!"

Joseph mumbled indistinctly in the depths of the cellar, but gave no intimation of ascending; so his master dived down to him, leaving me *vis-à-vis* the ruffianly bitch and a pair of grim shaggy sheep-dogs, who shared with her a jealous guardianship over all my movements. Not anxious to come in contact with their fangs, I sat still; but, imagining they would scarcely understand tacit insults, I unfortunately indulged in winking and making faces at the trio, and some turn of my physiognomy so irritated madam, that she suddenly broke into a fury, and leapt on my knees. I flung her back and hastened to interpose the table between us. This proceeding roused the whole hive. Half a dozen four-footed fiends, of various sizes and ages, issued from hidden dens to the common centre. I felt my heels and coat-laps peculiar subjects of assault; and, parrying off the larger combatants as effectually as I could with the poker, I was constrained to demand, aloud, assistance from some of the household in establishing peace.

Mr. Heathcliff and his man climbed the cellar steps with vexatious phlegm : I don't think they moved one second faster than usual though the hearth was an absolute tempest of worrying and yelping. Happily, an inhabitant of the kitchen made more dispatch : a lusty dame, with tucked-up gown, bare arms, and fire-flushed cheeks, rushed into the midst of us flourishing a frying-pan : and used that weapon, and her tongue, to such purpose, that the storm subsided magically, and she only remained, heaving like a sea after a high wind, when the master entered on the scene.

"What the devil is the matter?" he asked, eyeing me in a manner I could ill endure after this inhospitable treatment.

"What the devil, indeed!" I muttered. "The herd of possessed swine could have had no worse spirits in them than those animals of yours, sir. You might as well leave a stranger with a brood of tigers!"

"They won't meddle with persons who touch nothing," he remarked, putting the bottle before me, and restoring the displaced table. "The dogs do right to be vigilant. Take a glass of wine?"

"No, thank you."

"Not bitten, are you?"

"If I had been, I would have set my signet on the biter."

Heathcliff's countenance relaxed into a grin.

"Come, come," he said, "you are flurried, Mr. Lockwood. Here, take a little wine. Guests are so exceedingly rare in this house that I and my dogs, I am willing to own, hardly know how to receive them. Your health, sir !"

I bowed and returned the pledge; beginning to feel that it would be foolish to sit sulking for the misbehaviour of a pack of curs : besides, I felt loath to yield the fellow further amusement at my expense, since his humour took that turn.

From the moment when Lockwood flung the bitch back and roused the whole hive against him, his almost defenceless attitude is registered by a noticeable change in the orientation of the sentences. Either the passive mood of a verb or a semi-passive form of expression is used for describing Lockwood: "*I felt my heels and coat-laps* peculiar subjects of attack"; "*I was constrained* to demand, aloud, assistance." Upon the entrance of the cook and her magical subdual of the storm, we lose sight of Lockwood altogether, as is natural, and when he reappears, it is in keeping with his rather inglorious position that he is made to speak of himself in the accusative case. " 'What the devil is the matter?' he [Heathcliff] asked, eyeing *me*." The interval between his fright and feeling that it would be foolish to sit sulking is well indicated by Lockwood's answers, "No, thank you"; "If I had been, I would have set my signet on the biter," being set down on the page without the usual accompanying "I said" or "I replied." This not only suggests curtness but it marks an alteration of temper, the rage of "I muttered" quietening down through a midway sort of indifference to a resumption of good manners: "I bowed and returned the pledge."

The above passages bring us to the end of the first chapter. It is unnecessary to take the reader of this pamphlet in detail through the remaining introductory part, Chapters II and III and the beginning of Chapter IV. These continue Lockwood's account of his experiences at Wuthering Heights, his second visit there culminating in his night of nightmare and terrifying glimpse into Heathcliff's tortured soul, and his return to Thrushcross Grange, exhausted, to be the recipient, through several weeks of illness, of his housekeeper's history of the past. The technique throughout is the same as that so far examined; if the reader doubts this statement, he should pursue the analysis and in particular study the passage, in Chapter III, beginning: "This time, I remembered I was lying in the oak closet, and I heard distinctly the gusty wind, and the driving of the snow." Therein he will find, as indeed he will find in whatever passage he turns to, the same telling accent upon centres of movement and the same direct impressionism, which I have compared, and not without reason, to the stage-furniture maker's craft. The author of *Wuthering Heights* was first and foremost a spectator of events, an observer of drama from the outside. Even when the drama was psychological, it came more natural to that author to relate it as observed by someone than as occurring straightforwardly. Hence, in the history of Heathcliff's and Catherine's passion for one another, destructive of themselves and of much else besides, we get Mrs. Dean, who tells the tale, interposed between us and the characters of the book, and Mrs. Dean's occasional understudies, Zillah and Isabella, and finally Lockwood, in the role of a reporter of Mrs. Dean's own words. This interposition of an eye-witness, and, be it noted, an eye-witness not of present happenings but of events long past, somewhat differentiates the technique of the main part of the book from that of the opening chapters, but does not alter it essentially. The interposition is itself a device, though a primitive and clumsy one, for enhancing the reality of the story. "I was there"; "I saw it with my own eyes"; "I heard that very conversation," a narrative in the first person singular carries all these assurances with it and so helps to build up certainty in the mind of the reader. It is also, of course, an easy form in which to write. This consideration was evidently the one which weighed most with the writer of *Wuthering Heights*, for what with the narrative changing hands several times and there being always a recipient of the narrative to reckon with as well as a narrator, the book is not easy to read. Also, the point of view of the narrator is sometimes painfully obtrusive. Consider, for instance, Mrs. Dean's account of the last meeting between Heathcliff and Catherine on the eve of Catherine's death. There has been a savage, bitter conversation between them until Catherine makes an appeal, when comes an intensely moving passage:

> In her eagerness she rose and supported herself on the arm of the chair. At that earnest appeal he turned to her, looking absolutely desperate. His eyes wide, and wet at last, flashed fiercely on her; his breast heaved convulsively. An instant they held asunder, and then how they met I hardly saw, but Catherine made a spring, and he caught her, and they were locked in an embrace from which I thought my mistress would never be released alive: in fact, to my eyes, she seemed directly insensible.

It should be noticed how realization of the ultimate union of Heathcliff and Catherine is heightened by the singling out, in the first instance, of their actions. This effect is added to by the plural pronoun "they" being reserved for describing the last stage only of their wild embrace. The next sentences jar:

> . . . He flung himself into the nearest seat, and on my approaching hurriedly to ascertain if she had fainted, he gnashed at me, and foamed like a mad dog, and gathered her to him with greedy jealousy. I did not feel as if I were in the company of a creature of my own species: it appeared that he would not understand, though I spoke to him; so I stood off, and held my tongue, in great perplexity.

The reader, to say the least of it, wishes Mrs. Dean further. Her callousness (again noticeable later where she remarks: "At least, I suppose the weeping was on both sides; as it seemed Heathcliff *could* weep on a great occasion like this") is more hideously in the limelight than Heathcliff's frantic state. This lapse into vulgar consternation on her part is the more repellent because that sensitive description of the meeting has just been put into her mouth. Besides, her consternation is tainted; she has been the main instrument in bringing about the meeting. She cannot expect the reader suddenly to withdraw sympathy from the lovers in order to share her concern at the scene which through her guilty contrivance is taking place.

But this painful interruption of the reader's sympathies is the inevitable consequence of the primitive method of telling a story adopted in *Wuthering Heights*. Mrs. Dean, who is primarily a bare recorder of events, introduced by the writer in order to facilitate the work of composition, is also given a part to play in the story which is being told. And not a minor part, by any means. She it is whose partial, uncertain sympathies with the chief actors determine the actual progress of the story; her typical, but none the less fundamentally time-serving, habits of mind and actions are the wheels of fate. Her fitness to be a bare recorder is therefore suspect; the reader cannot take her impartiality for granted, he is constantly having to discount what she says. This is a drawback, from the point of view of literary aesthetics, though the majority of readers may not mind it, may indeed be oblivious of the fact that Mrs. Dean's version is not necessarily the whole truth. It must also be admitted that the drawback is more than occasionally balanced by the increase of verisimilitude imparted to the scene by Mrs. Dean's presence and palpitating concern. In the scene just referred to, the reader's tension as to the outcome of the meeting is enormously added to by Mrs. Dean's account of how uncomfortable she grew, as the afternoon wore fast away and at length she saw the Thrushcross Grange household returning from Gimmerton church, and finally Mr. Linton himself strolling up the drive. The reader is, of course, by this time identified with her, or at least with her anxiety to get Heathcliff out of the way before he

N

is discovered, and whenever this happens there is no denying the dramatic value of Mrs. Dean's presence and comments, or the extra substantiality thereby imparted to the scene.

To come now to the technique of the main part of the book as affected by Mrs. Dean's narration of the story to Lockwood, including what other people had, in their turn, narrated to her. The difference between this and the technique of the introductory chapters arises solely from the necessity of having to deal with events in perspective. Mrs. Dean is looking backwards, over a period of thirty years; though this fact of retrospect is often hidden by her extraordinary recollection of detail (emotional as well as material) which brings the reader close up to all the crucial scenes. These scenes succeed one another rapidly and are connected by stretches of narrative summarizing intermediate events with masterly cogency and a vividness that eliminates all sense of summary, transforming all these strips of summarizing narrative themselves into series of smaller scenes. In fact, no big scene is staged until the middle of Chapter VI, if we except the boy Heathcliff's account to Nelly Dean of his and Catherine's night escapade to the Grange when they were caught spying on the young Lintons through the drawing-room window. The reader, however, does not notice this; he is as interested as Lockwood was in the history of Wuthering Heights from that fine summer morning to which Mrs. Dean's memory goes back as she starts her tale.

Before I came to live here, she commenced . . . I was almost always at Wuthering Heights; because my mother had nursed Mr. Hindley Earnshaw, that was Hareton's father, and I got used to playing with the children: I ran errands too, and helped to make hay, and hung about the farm ready for anything that anybody would set me to. One fine summer morning—it was the beginning of harvest, I remember—Mr. Earnshaw, the old master, came downstairs, dressed for a journey; and after he had told Joseph what was to be done during the day, he turned to Hindley, and Cathy, and me—for I sat eating my porridge with them—and he said, speaking to his son, "Now, my bonny man, I'm going to Liverpool today, what shall I bring you? You may choose what you like: only let it be little, for I shall walk there and back: sixty miles each way, that is a long spell!" Hindley named a fiddle, and then he asked Miss Cathy; she was hardly six years old, but she could ride any horse in the stable, and she chose a whip. He did not forget me; for he had a kind heart, though he was rather severe sometimes. He promised to bring me a pocketful of apples and pears, and then he kissed his children, goodbye, and set off.

It seemed a long while to us all—the three days of his absence—and often did little Cathy ask when he would be home. Mrs. Earnshaw expected him by supper-time, on the third evening, and she put the meal off hour after hour; there were no signs of his coming, however, and at last the children got tired of running down to the gate to look. Then it grew dark; she would have had them to bed, but they begged sadly to be allowed to stay up; and, just about eleven o'clock, the door-latch was raised quietly, and in stept the master. He threw himself into a chair, laughing and groaning, and bid them all stand off, for he was nearly killed—he would not have such another walk for the three kingdoms.

"And at the end of it, to be flighted to death!" he said, opening his great-coat, which he held bundled up in his arms. "See here, wife! I was never so beaten with anything in my life: but you must e'en take it as a gift of God; though it's as dark almost as if it came from the devil."

We crowded round, and over Miss Cathy's head I had a peep at a dirty, ragged, black-haired child; big enough both to walk and talk: indeed, its face looked older than Catherine's; yet, when it was set on its feet, it only stared round, and repeated over and over again some gibberish, that nobody could understand. I was frightened, and Mrs. Earnshaw was ready to fling it out of doors: she did fly up, asking how he could fashion to bring that gipsy brat into the house, when they had their own bairns to feed and fend for? What he meant to do with it, and whether he were mad? The master tried to explain the matter; but he was really half dead with fatigue, and all that I could make out, amongst her scolding, was a tale of his seeing it starving, and houseless, and as good as dumb, in the streets of Liverpool; where he picked it up and inquired for its owner. Not a soul knew to whom it belonged, he said; and his money and time being both limited, he thought it better to take it home with him at once, than run into vain expenses there: because he was determined he would not leave it as he found it. Well, the conclusion was that my mistress grumbled herself calm; and Mr. Earnshaw told me to wash it, and give it clean things, and let it sleep with the children.

Hindley and Cathy contented themselves with looking and listening till peace was restored: then, both began searching their father's pockets for the presents he had promised them. The former was a boy of fourteen, but when he drew out what had been a fiddle, crushed to morsels in the great-coat, he blubbered aloud; and Cathy, when she learnt the master had lost her whip in attending on the stranger, showed her humour by grinning and spitting at the stupid little thing; earning for her pains a sound blow from her father to teach her cleaner manners. They entirely refused to have it in bed with them, or even in their room; and I had no more sense, so I put it on the landing of the stairs, hoping it might be gone on the morrow. By chance, or else attracted by hearing his voice, it crept to Mr. Earnshaw's door, and there he found it on quitting his chamber. Inquiries were made as to how it got there; I was obliged to confess, and in recompense for my cowardice and inhumanity was sent out of the house.

This was Heathcliff's first introduction to the family. On coming back a few days afterwards (for I did not consider my banishment perpetual) I found they had christened him "Heathcliff": it was the name of a son who died in childhood, and it has served him ever since, both for Christian and surname.

In this passage, picture follows picture with cinematographic effect. Almost every sentence is a sketch. The sketching broadens; a scene develops, disappears into more sketches which flash into another scene. The scenes are lit by dialogue, verbatim or reported, but there is the same vivid, swift touch whether sketch or fuller picture is being drawn. The reader's interest never flags; he is never tempted to skip. The cogency at times is almost too tight. There are a few characteristic grammatical slips because of this. Take this passage, for instance, following Mrs. Dean's account, in Chapter VII, of her search for Heathcliff on Christmas Eve and attempt to smarten him up for the festivities. She found him, sullen, in the stable, but he would not respond.

I waited five minutes, but getting no answer left him. Catherine supped with her brother and sister-in-law: Joseph and I joined at an unsociable meal, seasoned with reproofs on one side and sauciness on the other. His cake and cheese remained on the table all night for the fairies. He managed to continue work till nine o'clock, and then marched dumb and dour to his chamber.

The "His" and "He" in the last two sentences refer, of course, to Heathcliff, who is so centrally in the writer's mind for the moment that the intermediate mention of Joseph, to whom, strictly, "His" is referable, has been overlooked. This sort of slip, due to sharp focusing and instinct for straightforward narrative, occurs several times.

For another example of vivid summary which I have likened to a swift series of snapshots connecting the longer-exposed scenes, see the passage preceding Nelly Dean's descriptions of finding Heathcliff in the stable on Christmas Eve.

After playing lady's maid to the new comer, [i.e. Cathy just returned from her stay with the Lintons at Thrushcross Grange] and putting my cakes in the oven, and making the house and kitchen cheerful with great fires, befitting Christmas eve, I prepared to sit down and amuse myself by singing carols, all alone; regardless of Joseph's affirmations that he considered the merry tunes I chose as next door to songs. He had retired to private prayer in his chamber, and Mr. and Mrs. Earnshaw were engaging Missy's attention by sundry gay trifles bought for her to present to the little Lintons, as an acknowledgment of their kindness. They had invited them to spend the morrow at Wuthering Heights, and the invitation had been accepted, on one condition: Mrs. Linton begged that her darlings might be kept carefully apart from that "naughty swearing boy."

It should be noticed that the reference to the Lintons and their coming visit to Wuthering Heights is no casual digression but is required to explain the display of the presents; that the writer has no intention of unnecessarily departing from the direct line of the narrative is shown by the opening of the next sentence:

Under these circumstances [that is to say the circumstances described in the beginning of the passage here quoted, *not* the circumstances of the coming of the Lintons on the morrow] I remained solitary. I smelt the rich scent of the heating spices: and admired the shining kitchen utensils, the polished clock, decked in holly, the silver mugs ranged on a tray ready to be filled with mulled ale for supper; and above all, the speckless purity of my particular care—the scoured and well-swept floor. I gave due applause to every object, and then I remembered how old Earnshaw used to come in when all was tidied, and call me a cant lass, and slip a shilling into my hand as a Christmas box; and from that I went on to think of his fondness for Heathcliff, and his dread lest he should suffer neglect after death had removed him; and that naturally led me to consider the poor lad's situation now, and from singing I changed my mind to crying. It struck me soon, however, there would be more sense in endeavouring to repair some of his wrongs than shedding tears over them : I got up and walked into the court to seek him.

The cogency here is typical of the whole narrative. I have not selected the passage purposely. Page after page gives such examples. There are no casual digressions in *Wuthering Heights*; every divergence from the main course of the narrative is motivated, and, its purpose being effected, that main course is immediately resumed. The writer was as conscientious to avoid irrelevant statement as to be exact and consistent throughout the story with regard to the ages of the characters and the periods of events. This conscientiousness as to dates, and as to legal knowledge concerning the devolution of the Thrushcross Grange property at Edgar Linton's death, was pointed out by Mr. Sanger (C.P.S.) in his essay, "The Structure of Wuthering Heights." The author's grip upon such details is, indeed, all of a piece with the book's astonishing cogency and economy of statement. A proof of that author's deliberate aim to steer a straight course is afforded in Chapter XI. The chapter begins with an account by Mrs. Dean of a fearful visit which she made to the farm after the returned Heathcliff had taken up his abode there. Her hope was to get a glimpse of the wretched Hindley, but she only succeeded in seeing the child, Hareton, fast degenerating under Heathcliff's influence into a young ruffian. At the end of Chapter X, she had been relating Isabella Linton's infatuation for Heathcliff and his ominous musing over that, and, evidently fearing that she might be guilty of rambling, she concludes her account of the visit by saying:

"This is not much connected with Miss Isabella's affair; except that it urged me to resolve further on mounting vigilant guard, and doing my utmost to check the spread of such bad influence at the Grange." She then proceeds to tell of Heathcliff's prompt advances to Isabella.

Now this cogency and economy of statement, this scrupulous concentration on the significant events in the story, is only another form of the technique of dramatic incisiveness which has been pointed out in the passages taken from the introductory chapters of the book. In those chapters, Lockwood, the diarist, is facing the immediate present, is *barging* into it, to use a vulgar expression, but one which happens to fit the way he behaves on his visits to the farm. He cannot see ahead; there is no time dimension to reckon with in describing his experience; all that he is concerned to convey to the reader is what is taking place where, at the moment, he is. But in the main part of the book, the present is *behind* Lockwood; he is looking the other way, under Mrs. Dean's guidance, across and through a long period of years. It is not enough that he should see past scenes vividly; his attention must also be guided to crucial, determining events. The seizure of these, the emphasis placed on their relationship to each other, and on the links between them, is the equivalent, in a survey of the past, of that accent upon movement which, in the description of a scene, is essential to make it vivid. Crucial events, in short, may be regarded as the hinges of action in a story, and cogency and stress upon these are the incisive tools with which a writer must work, if the story is to be dramatically told. The author of *Wuthering Heights* used these tools as effectively as she (or he) employed the technique in the art of scene-making which has been already examined.

The main part of the book shows the latter technique still being used, but alongside or supplemented by the former; and the combination of the two results in a literary masterpiece, the dramatic intensity of which has perhaps never been surpassed. At the close of the story, the reader finds himself once more gazing with Lockwood on events at the farm a year and a half later than those with which he was faced at the opening of the book. Again, through Mrs. Dean, the story of the year and a half's happenings is unfolded to Lockwood, who thereupon makes his exit from Wuthering Heights as self-effacingly as his former entrance there had been intrusive. Returning to Thrush-cross Grange, he goes out of his way to visit the churchyard. He seeks and soon discovers the three headstones, on the slope next the moor; "the middle one grey, and half buried in heath; Edgar Linton's only harmonized by the turf, and moss creeping up its foot; Heathcliff's still bare." It was a September evening and there was moonlight. The curtain falls on a scene empty of drama and one whose utter quietude is perfectly drawn. It is drawn with the same technique as before noticed, only here there is no movement to be stressed, but the *opposite* of movement. Lockwood's impressions are of almost impalpable things.

> I lingered round them, under that benign sky: watched the moths fluttering among the heath and harebells; listened to the soft wind breathing through the grass; and wondered how any one could ever imagine unquiet slumbers for the sleepers in that quiet earth.

The Structure of
"Wuthering Heights"*

C. P. SANGER

B Y COMMON consent *Wuthering Heights* is a remarkable book. I do not propose to discuss its literary merits, but to confine myself to the humbler task of investigating its structure, which presents certain peculiarities. Whether this is worth doing I do not know, but I found that it added to my interest in the book and made the tale much more vivid for me.

The main theme is how a sort of human cuckoo, called Heathcliff, sets out with success to acquire all the property of two families, the Earnshaws and the Lintons. The tale is a fairly complicated one, and the incidents extend over a period of more than thirty years. Stated as baldly and shortly as I can, the plot is as follows: Mr. and Mrs. Earnshaw live at Wuthering Heights, a farmhouse on a Yorkshire moor. They have two children, a son called Hindley and a daughter Catherine. One day Mr. Earnshaw, who has been to Liverpool on business, brings home a waif he has picked up there. This waif, Heathcliff, is brought up at Wuthering Heights. Not long after, Mrs. Earnshaw dies. Heathcliff is Mr. Earnshaw's favourite; he is also great friends with Catherine, but Hindley, who is older, bullies him. At last, Hindley is sent off to college. When Mr.

* A paper originally read to the Heretics, Cambridge. First published as Hogarth Essay number XIX (1926). Now reprinted by kind permission of the Hogarth Press Ltd.

O

Earnshaw dies, Hindley returns for the funeral, bringing with him a young wife. He takes possession, ill-treats Heathcliff, thrusts him into the position of a mere servant, and allows him no more education. But Catherine and Heathcliff have remained great friends, and one Sunday they go for a walk, and out of curiosity look at Thrushcross Grange, a gentleman's house in a park four miles off where Mr. and Mrs. Linton live. Catherine and Heathcliff peep in through the drawing-room window and see the two Linton children—Edgar and Isabella. The Lintons, hearing Heathcliff and Catherine and taking them for robbers, let the bulldog loose on them; the dog seizes Catherine and hurts her ankle badly. She is taken in and looked after at Thrushcross Grange for five weeks, and returns to Wuthering Heights elegantly dressed. Heathcliff, who is very dirty and untidy, is ashamed. The next day the two Lintons come to dinner; Heathcliff behaves ill and is punished by Hindley. The next year Hindley's wife gives birth to a son—Hareton. She, however, is consumptive and does not survive long. In despair at her death Hindley takes to drink. When Catherine is fifteen Edgar Linton proposes to her. She accepts him, feeling all the time that she is doing wrong because she loves Heathcliff. She tells Hareton's nurse, Ellen Dean, about it; Heathcliff overhears part of the conversation, runs off and vanishes. Catherine is distracted by this, gets fever, and when convalescent goes to stay at Thrushcross Grange. Her host and hostess, Mr. and Mrs. Linton, both catch the fever and die. This may be considered the end of the first stage of the story. The elder generation are all dead. The next generation are all alive— Hindley and Catherine at Wuthering Heights, Edgar and Isabella at Thrushcross Grange. Hindley's wife is dead, but his son Hareton—the only representative of the third generation— is alive. Heathcliff has disappeared. His passion for Catherine and his revenge is the main theme of the root of the story.

Catherine in due course marries Edgar and goes to live at Thrushcross Grange. After six months of happiness, Heathcliff, who has meanwhile mysteriously got some education and money, reappears. He sets himself to ruin Hindley, who gambles and drinks. He also finds that Isabella is in love with him, and decides to marry her to get her money. One day, after a violent scene between Heathcliff and Edgar, Catherine goes on hunger strike and gets brain fever. Isabella elopes with Heathcliff, who treats her abominably, and finally brings her back to Wuthering Heights. One Sunday while Edgar is at church, Heathcliff comes to see Catherine. There is a passionate scene. That night Catherine gives birth to a daughter and dies. On the night after the funeral, Hindley tries to kill Heathcliff but is nearly killed by him. Isabella escapes from Wuthering Heights and goes to the South of England, where she gives birth to a sickly child named Linton Heathcliff. Soon after this Hindley dies of drink, and Heathcliff is left in possession of Wuthering Heights with Hareton, whom, out of revenge for the way he was treated as a boy, he brings up as a mere brute. At this stage there is a long gap in the story. Edgar's daughter, who is also called Catherine, lives with him at Thrushcross Grange; Isabella's son, Linton, lives in the South of England with her. Catherine is kept in ignorance of both her cousins Linton and Hareton.

Edgar hears that Isabella is dying and goes to see her. Catherine in his absence goes to Penistone Crags, and in doing so has to pass Wuthering Heights, where she sees Hareton. On Isabella's death, Edgar comes home with Linton, but Heathcliff claims him, and he is taken to Wuthering Heights. Catherine is not allowed by Edgar, her father, to go there. One day, after some time, Catherine on a walk meets Heathcliff and Hareton and goes to Wuthering Heights, where she sees her cousin, Linton. Catherine and Linton correspond secretly. The correspondence is detected and stopped. Catherine's father, Edgar, becomes ill. Heathcliff meets Catherine and tells her that Linton is seriously ill. She goes to see him, and many times visits him secretly. One day, just before her father dies, she is kidnapped by Heathcliff and forced to marry Linton. Soon after Linton dies, having made a will leaving all his personal property to his father, Heathcliff. Heathcliff takes possession of Thrushcross Grange, and lets it to Mr. Lockwood, who tells the story. But Heathcliff dies soon after, and Hareton and Catherine marry.

How is a long story like this to be told? How is the reader's interest to be excited? How is the tale to be kept together? How are we to be made to feel the lapse of time without being pestered by dates? How far did the authoress accurately visualize the ages of the characters in the different incidents, the topography, and so on? And how did Heathcliff succeed in getting the property? These are the questions I attempt to answer.

The most obvious thing about the structure of the story which deals with three generations is the symmetry of the pedigree. Mr. and Mrs. Earnshaw at Wuthering Heights and Mr. and Mrs. Linton at Thrushcross Grange each have one son and one daughter. Mr. Linton's son marries Mr. Earnshaw's daughter, and their only child Catherine marries successively her two cousins—Mr. Linton's grandson and Mr. Earnshaw's grandson. See the pedigree on the next page.

In actual life I have never come across a pedigree of such absolute symmetry. I shall have to refer to this pedigree again later. It is a remarkable piece of symmetry in a tempestuous book.

The method adopted to arouse the reader's interest and to give vividness and reality to the tale is one which has been used with great success by Joseph Conrad. But it requires great skill.

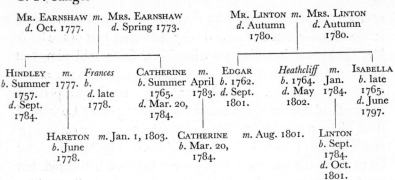

MR. EARNSHAW *m.* MRS. EARNSHAW
    d. Oct. 1777.   *d.* Spring 1773.

MR. LINTON *m.* MRS. LINTON
    d. Autumn   *d.* Autumn
      1780.   1780.

HINDLEY   *m.*   *Frances*   CATHERINE   *m.*   EDGAR   *Heathcliff*   *m.*   ISABELLA
b. Summer 1777. *b.*   *b.* Summer April *b.* 1762.   *b.* 1764. Jan.   *b.* late
    1757.   *d.* late   1765. 1783. *d.* Sept.   *d.* May 1784.   1765.
d. Sept.   1778.   *d.* Mar. 20,   1801.   1802.   *d.* June
  1784.   1784.   1797.

HARETON   *m.* Jan. 1, 1803.   CATHERINE   *m.* Aug. 1801.   LINTON
b. June   *b.* Mar. 20,   *b.* Sept.
  1778.   1784.   1784.
                                                              d. Oct.
                                                              1801.

After Edgar Linton's death, Mr. Lockwood, the narrator, takes Thrushcross Grange for a year. He goes to call on his landlord, Heathcliff, at Wuthering Heights, and is puzzled to find there a *farouche* young woman and an awkward boor. At first he supposes Catherine to be Heathcliff's wife; when told she is his daughter-in-law, he then supposes that Hareton is Heathcliff's son, and has again to be corrected. He, and the reader, are naturally puzzled at this strange trio. Lockwood calls again, and is forced to spend the night because of a heavy fall of snow. In his room he finds some books with the name Catherine Earnshaw and Catherine Linton, and a sort of diary of Catherine's in a childish hand which gives a vivid picture of the situation just after her father's death. Mr. Lockwood has a nightmare in which Catherine's spirit comes to the window, and he also witnesses a strange scene of Heathcliff imploring Catherine's spirit. Our interest cannot fail now to be excited. What is this strange man and this strange *ménage*? Who was this Catherine who died years before? What were her relations with Heathcliff? Naturally, Lockwood is much intrigued. On his way back next day he catches a chill and becomes ill. To pass the time he asks Ellen Dean, the housekeeper at Thrushcross Grange, what she knows about the family at Wuthering Heights. She, who was first Hareton's nurse and then the younger Catherine's, tells him the story of the past thirty years in considerable detail. So that during the major part of the book Mr. Lockwood is telling us what Ellen Dean told him, but sometimes, also, what Ellen Dean told him that someone else— for instance, Isabella—had told her. Only a small part, perhaps one-tenth of the book, consists of direct narrative by Lockwood from his own knowledge. But such a scheme may be confusing, and it is easy to muddle the time. Did Emily Brontë realize and let us know the dates when each event happened? She did, but not by giving them directly. Look again at the pedigree. The dates there have all been derived from the book, yet only one is directly stated. What first brought me to study the book more closely was when I noticed that the first word in the book was a date—1801. I thought this must have some significance. Similarly, the first word of Chapter XXXII is 1802. Apart from this, only one other date is given directly. In the last sentence of Chapter VII, Ellen Dean says, "I will be content to pass on to the next summer—the summer of 1778, that is, nearly twenty-three years ago." This gives no further information, as 1801 is twenty-three years after 1778, but in the first sentence of the next chapter she tells us that Hareton was born in June. This is how I get June 1778 for Hareton's birth in the pedigree. But what about the rest of the dates, not only those in the pedigree but of all the incidents in the story? There are a considerable number (perhaps nearly a hundred) indications of various kinds to help us—intervals of time, ages of characters, the months, the harvest moon, the last grouse, and so forth, and we learn, incidentally, that the younger Catherine's birthday was on 20th March. Sometimes, too, we know the day of the week— thus Ellen Dean will remember something which happened on a Sunday, or on a Christmas Eve. Taking all these indications, it is, I think, possible to ascertain the year, and, in most cases, the month of the year in which every event takes place—

also the ages of the various characters, except, naturally, there is a slight doubt as to Heathcliff, because no one knows his exact age when he was found by Mr. Earnshaw. But one has to go warily and consider all the indications together, for there is a curious subtlety that sometimes the characters are described as *looking* some ages which are not exact. Thus Lockwood when he first describes them says that Heathcliff was about forty and Catherine did not look seventeen. In fact, Catherine was seventeen and three-quarters and Heathcliff cannot have been more than thirty-eight. It would be too tedious to state the process by which I have discovered each date (see Appendix). But I will give one or two illustrations. We already know that Hareton was born in June 1778; we are told that he was nearly five when Catherine Earnshaw married Edgar Linton, so that the marriage was before June 1783. But Heathcliff returned in September after they had been happily married for six months. Thus the marriage was in April 1783. We are told that the scene that led to Catherine's death was a Sunday in the March after Heathcliff's return, and that her daughter, Catherine, was born about midnight, and the mother died two hours later. Later on we learn that Catherine's birthday was the 20th (and that this was also treated as the day of her mother's death). Hence Catherine died at 2 a.m. on Monday, 20th March 1784.

I will give only one other instance. Lockwood begins his account in 1801; it is snowy weather, which might be in January or February or in November or December. But he returns in 1802 before his year's tenancy is out. Hence the story begins at the end of 1801. A Michaelmas tenancy begins on the 10th October—not on 29th September—because when the calendar was reformed eleven days were left out. Therefore, the story begins after 10th October 1801. Now after Lockwood has been ill three weeks Heathcliff sends him some grouse, the last of the season. Since the Game Act, 1831, grouse may not be shot after 10th

December, so we may take this as about the date for the last grouse. Thus the story begins about the middle of November, and this fits pretty well with the later indications. That is sufficient to illustrate the process. Sometimes it is only by fitting together several indications, each rather vague, that one can find the month. There is, however, one curious fact. We can ascertain Hindley's age. Now Ellen Dean was of the same age. She was his foster sister, and the doctor also refers to her as being of the same age as Hindley. Yet she makes two mistakes about her own age. Middle-aged people do, of course, make mistakes about their age, and these slips may have been intentional on the part of Emily Brontë, but, if so, it seems to me a little over-subtle.

The topography is equally precise. On going from Thrushcross Grange to the village of Gimmerton a highway branches off to the moor on the left. There is a stone pillar there. Thrushcross Grange lies to the south-west, Gimmerton to the east, and Wuthering Heights to the north. The distance from Thrushcross Grange to Wuthering Heights is four miles, and Penistone Crags lie a mile and a half farther on. It was half an hour from Gimmerton to Thrushcross Grange.

The botany is sure to be correct. Emily Brontë loved the country. I was a little surprised to find an ash tree in bud as early as 20th March, but then I realized that it was not on the moor but in the park at Thrushcross Grange, which lay low and was no doubt sheltered.

I now come to the final problem. Heathcliff schemed to get all the property of both the Earnshaws and the Lintons. How did he do it? Emily Brontë clearly had a considerable knowledge of the law. We know the source of George Eliot's use of a base fee for the plot of Felix Holt. We do not know the source of Jane Austen's unerring grasp of the law of real property; but she lived among people who had settled estates and could easily have obtained it. But how Emily Brontë acquired her knowledge I cannot guess. There is also this difficulty. *Wuthering Heights* was written in the eighteen-forties. It was published in 1847. But the period of the tale is from 1771 to 1803. The Inheritance Act of 1834, the Wills Act of 1837, and, I think, the Game Act of 1831, had changed the law. Did Emily Brontë apply the law at the time she wrote or that at the period of the tale? In one case, as we shall see, she used the earlier law.

Novelists sometimes make their plots depend on the law and use legal terms. But they frequently make mistakes and sometimes are absurd as Trollope is in *Orley Farm*. What is remarkable about *Wuthering Heights* is that the ten or twelve legal references are, I think, sufficient to enable us to ascertain the various legal processes by which Heathcliff obtained the property. It is not a simple matter. There was a fundamental difference between the law of land (real property) and that of money and goods (personal property).

Let us begin with Wuthering Heights. The Earnshaws were farmers and not likely to have their estate settled. The property had been in their family since 1500. We may take it then that Mr. Earnshaw was owner in fee-simple, that is in effect absolute owner, of Wuthering Heights, and was not likely to have possessed any investments. It is more likely that there was a mortgage on the house and farm. On Mr. Earnshaw's death the land descended to Hindley as his heir-at-law. There is no mention of a will. The personal property, which, probably, was only the farming stock and the furniture, would go equally to his children, Hindley and Catherine, subject to the payment of his debts out of it. On Catherine's marriage Edgar would have become entitled to her personal property. Now Hindley drinks and gambles away all he has, and at his death the property is mortgaged up to the hilt. Heathcliff we find is the mortgagee. The personal property would also be liable to the debts. So that Heathcliff is mortgagee in possession and, for practical purposes, owner of all the Earnshaw property except any personalty that had gone to Catherine. This is all fairly simple; but it is more difficult when we come to the Linton property. They were landed gentry; they had a park, they had tenants. Mr. Linton, and Edgar after him, was a magistrate. Such people, generally, had a settlement of their land, and we find, in fact, that Mr. Linton had settled it by his will. To understand what happens it is necessary to go into the intricacies of real property law and to look at the pedigree.

I must explain very shortly the law of entails. What is called an estate tail is an estate which descends according to the following rules: (1) Males are preferred to females; (2) males take in order according to seniority of birth, but females take equally; (3) descendants represent their ancestor. In case of a conflict between them, rule (3) prevails. A tenant in tail of full age in possession could by means of a fictitious action (for which a deed was substituted by the Fines and Recoveries Act, 1833) bar the entail and obtain the fee-simple, which practically amounts to absolute ownership. By his will a testator could settle his land on living persons for life, but could not give life estates to the children of such persons who were not alive at the testator's death. Consequently, if he wanted to tie up his estate as long as possible, he gave life estates to such of his descendants as were living at his death, followed by estates tail to their children.

Now the settlement made by Mr. Linton's will must have been as follows: The estate was devised to Edgar, his only son, for life, then to Edgar's sons in tail; Edgar's daughters were passed over in favour of Mr. Linton's daughter, Isabella, who, presumably, had a life interest with remainder to her sons in tail. This is the usual form. Thus on Edgar Linton's death, Linton Heathcliff became tenant in tail in possession during the few weeks he survived his uncle. As a minor he could not bar the

entail. It is most improbable that he had an estate in fee-simple;
that would have been too unusual. Isabella might have had an
estate tail instead of a life interest. This is most improbable, but
if she did, her son, Linton Heathcliff, would have become
tenant in tail by descent, so the result is the same. Heathcliff
claims the property—by what right? Ellen Dean says that he
claimed and kept the Thrushcross Grange estate in his wife's
right and in his son's also. She adds: "I suppose, legally at any
rate, Catherine, destitute of cash and friends, cannot disturb his
possession." She is quite right in her suspicions. Even if Isabella
had had an estate tail, or even an estate in fee-simple, Heathcliff would not have had any right as husband to an estate for
life—the estate known as an estate by courtesy—because Isabella
was never in possession. And even if, which to my mind is not
possible, Linton Heathcliff had had an estate in fee-simple, his
father would not have been his heir before the Inheritance Act,
1833, because it was considered unnatural that an inheritance
should ascend directly; and, as Ellen Dean knows and states,
Linton Heathcliff as a minor could not dispose of his land by
will. There is no difficulty as to the personal property. Whatever Isabella had Heathcliff got by marrying her. There was no
Married Women's Property Act in these days. They eloped, so
there was no question of a marriage-settlement. Edgar Linton
had saved out of his rents to make a provision for his daughter,
Catherine. When dying he decides, in order to prevent Heathcliff getting at them, to alter his will so as to settle them on
Catherine for life and then for her children. The attorney for
whom he sends is, however, kept from going by Heathcliff, and
Edgar dies before his will is altered, so the money passes to
Catherine and then to her husband, Linton. He, though a
minor, could (before the year 1838) make a will of personalty.
He is induced or forced to do so, and leaves it all to Heathcliff.

Thus, at Heathcliff's death, the position seems to be that he has acquired all the personal property of both families: he is mortgagee in possession of Wuthering Heights, and is, though wrongfully, in possession of Thrushcross Grange, which he has let to Lockwood. He thinks of making a will but does not do so. What then happens on his death? He has no relations, so that his real property will escheat, and his personal property will go to the Crown as *bona vacantia*. What then becomes of Hareton and Catherine who, when the tale ends, are to be happily married on New Year's Day, 1803? At one time I thought this was the climax of the tragedy. These young people, ill-educated and incompetent, were to be left destitute. But that would be going too far. Catherine, as you will see from the pedigree, is the sole living descendant of Mr. Linton. In some way or other, I need not go through the various alternatives, she must have become entitled to Thrushcross Grange, which is plainly by far the most valuable property. Heathcliff had been mortgagee in possession of Wuthering Heights for eighteen years, but this was not long enough to obtain an absolute title by adverse possession. Hareton, as Hindley's heir, would be entitled to the equity of redemption. Now if Heathcliff, who managed well, properly accounted for his profits during the eighteen years as he could be made to do, it may well be that they were sufficient, if he was charged a proper occupation rent, to pay off the mortgage. So that Hareton would get the house and land unencumbered or, at any rate, only slightly burdened. The personal property was comparatively unimportant, and we can only hope that the Crown did not insist on its rights, if it knew of them, or that if it did insist, the happy couple could buy out the Crown's claim out of the rent which Lockwood, as we know, paid.

There is, so far as I know, no other novel in the world which it is possible to subject to an analysis of the kind I have tried to make. This in itself makes the book very unusual. Did the authoress carry all the dates in her head, or did she work with a calendar? Was 20th March 1784, for example, on a Monday? According to my calculations it was not, it was a Saturday, but I should like to have this confirmed by some competent chronologist; for if I am right, it shows that Emily Brontë did not use a calendar, and that nothing will be gained by finding out, for instance, the date of Easter in 1803.

However dull and technical the above details may be, they do, I believe, throw a light on the character of Emily Brontë and her book. German romances can hardly have been the source of her knowledge of English law. A great critic has spoken of the passionate chastity of the book; but the extreme care in realizing the ages of the characters at the time of each incident which is described seems to me a more unusual characteristic of a novel. It demonstrates the vividness of the author's imagination.

CHRONOLOGY OF WUTHERING HEIGHTS

CHAP.			
	1757,	before September	Hindley Earnshaw born.
	1762,	,,	Edgar Linton born.
	1764,	,,	Heathcliff born.
	1765,	summer	Catherine Earnshaw born.
	,,	late	Isabella Linton born.
IV.	1771,	summer, beginning of harvest	Heathcliff brought to Wuthering Heights.
	1773,	spring or early summer	Mrs. Earnshaw dies.
V.	1774,	October	Hindley sent to college.
	1777,		Hindley marries.
	,,	,,	Mr. Earnshaw dies.
VI.	,,	,,	Hindley returns with his wife.
III.	,,	October or November	The scene described by Catherine.
VI.	,,	November, third week, Sunday	Catherine and Heathcliff go to Thrushcross Grange.

CHAP.			
VII.	1777,	Christmas Eve	Catherine returns to W. H.
	,,	Christmas Day	The Lintons visit W. H.
VIII.	1778,	June	Hareton Earnshaw born.
	,,	late	Frances Earnshaw dies.
	1780,	summer	Edgar Linton calls at W. H. and proposes to Catherine.
IX.	,,	,,	Hindley returns drunk.
	,,	,,	Catherine tells Ellen about Edgar.
	,,	,,	Heathcliff goes off.
	,,	,,	Catherine gets wet through and catches fever.
	,,	autumn	Catherine, convalescent, goes to Thrushcross Grange. Mr. and Mrs. Linton catch the fever and die.
	1783,	April	Edgar marries Catherine.
X.	,,	September	Heathcliff returns and sees Catherine.
	,,	autumn	Isabella falls in love with Heathcliff, who visits Thrushcross Grange from time to time.
XI.	,,	December	Ellen Dean sees Hareton. Heathcliff kisses Isabella.
	1784,	January 6, Monday	Violent scene at Thrushcross Grange. Heathcliff is turned out and Catherine goes on hunger strike.
XII.	,,	January 10, Friday	Catherine delirious.
	,,	,, ,, 2 a.m.	Isabella elopes with Heathcliff.
XIII.	,,	March 13, Monday	The Heathcliffs return to W. H.
XIV.	,,	March 15, Wednesday	Ellen Dean goes to W. H.
XV.	,,	March 19, Sunday	Heathcliff sees Catherine : violent scene.
XVI.	,,	,, midnight	Catherine Linton born.
	,,	March 20, Monday, 2 a.m.	Catherine (the elder) dies.
	,,	March 21, Tuesday	Heathcliff puts a lock of hair in Catherine's locket.
	,,	March 24, Friday	Catherine's funeral.

CHAP.			
XVII.	1784,	same day, midnight	Heathcliff nearly kills Hindley, who tried to kill him.
	,,	March 25, Saturday	Isabella runs off.
	,,	September	Linton Heathcliff born.
	,,	September or October	Hindley Earnshaw dies. All his property is mortgaged to Heathcliff.
XVIII.	1797,	early June	Catherine goes to Penistone Crags and meets Hareton.
XIX.	,,	June	Isabella dies. Edgar brings back Linton Heathcliff.
XX.	,,	,,	Linton Heathcliff is taken to live at Wuthering Heights.
XXI.	1800,	March 20	Catherine and Ellen meet Hareton, and go to Wuthering Heights where they see Linton.
	,,	March or April	Catherine and Linton correspond.
XXII.	,,	late October or November	Catherine sees Heathcliff, who says that Linton is seriously ill.
XXIII.	,,	late October or November	Catherine and Ellen go to see Linton. Ellen catches cold and is ill for three weeks.
XXIV.	,,	November	During Ellen's illness Catherine visits Linton secretly.
XXV.	1801,	March 20	Edgar too ill to visit his wife's grave.
	,,	June	Edgar declining.
XXVI.	,,	August	Ellen and Catherine go to meet Linton.
	,,	August, Thursday, a week later	They are kidnapped.
	,,	Monday?	Catherine and Linton marry.
XXVII.	,,	August or September	Ellen is let out.
	,,	next Tuesday	Edgar is dying; he sends for Mr. Green, the lawyer, who does not come.
		harvest moon	Catherine escapes and comes to Thrushcross Grange.
XXVIII.	,,	Wednesday, 3 a.m.,	Edgar Linton dies.

CHAP.			
XXIX.	1801,	September, evening after the funeral	Heathcliff comes to the Grange and takes off Catherine.
XXX.	,,	October	Linton Heathcliff dies. Hareton tries to please Catherine.
I.	,,	late November	Lockwood calls at W. H.
II.	,,	next day	He calls again and has to stay the night. He finds Catherine's diary and sees Heathcliff's outburst.
	,,	next day	Leaves at eight. Catches cold.
IV.	,,	,,	Ellen Dean begins her story.
X.	,,	three weeks later	Heathcliff sends grouse.
	,,	one week later	Heathcliff calls.
XV.	1802,	January, one week later	Lockwood continues his account.
XXXI.	,,	January, 2nd week	Lockwood calls at W. H.
XXXII.	,,	beginning of February	Ellen goes to live at W. H.
	,,	March	Hareton has an accident.
	,,	Easter Monday	Catherine is nice to Hareton.
XXXIII.	,,	Easter Tuesday	Scene about altering garden.
	,,	(after March 18)	Heathcliff getting odd.
XXXIV.	,,	April	Heathcliff goes on hunger strike.
	,,	May	Heathcliff dies.
	,,	September	Lockwood visits Thrushcross Grange and Wuthering Heights.
XXXIV.	1803,	January 1	Catherine and Hareton marry.